THOSE WHO STAY

Curt Stephenson

authorHOUSE®

AuthorHouse™
1663 Liberty Drive, Suite 200
Bloomington, IN 47403
www.authorhouse.com
Phone: 1-800-839-8640

First published by AuthorHouse 10/15/2008

ISBN: 978-1-4389-0029-2 (sc)
ISBN: 978-1-4389-0030-8 (hc)

Library of Congress Control Number: 2008906278

Printed in the United States of America
Bloomington, Indiana

This book is printed on acid-free paper.

Front cover image courtesy of the Detroit Free Press

ACKNOWLEDGEMENTS

First and foremost, I would like to thank my wife, Kate. She had to endure these stories over and over again for the last three decades without the benefit of being a Michigan graduate or a football fan. Special thanks to all of my teammates and coaches' of those great Michigan teams. Our experiences can never be replaced or taken from us. I owe eternal gratitude to Bo Schembechler because, without him, none of this would have been possible.

THOSE WHO STAY

This is a simple story. It is a written account of some of the stories from when I walked on to the University of Michigan Football team. How I came to play for the school. The question is always asked, why write a book? The answer is two fold. I signed up for The Wolverine a few years back , primarily because I am a Michigan football fan and I wanted to keep up with what was happening to the team. This is hard to do when you live 2500 miles away, running a business and raising a family, so The Wolverine seemed a logical choice.

The second reason is extremely selfish. I love my family. They have grown up around me and for decades have been showered with my life in Michigan football. They know their old man and have heard him talk about how great my experiences were during that time of my life. I want them to experience everything that I went through. I know deep in my heart they can't, but I felt that I could give them a taste.

One of my children is coming as close as you can get as he has traveled a similar path and it does my heart good to know that he too is living that life to a certain extent. Maybe writing my experiences will give my children some insight what their dad went through and why he loves Michigan football so much.

Back to The Wolverine. This is a publication that follows Michigan Football. They have both a magazine and web site. I was on their web site and during the recruitment of my son by the University of Michigan, I wrote about the process to the other subscribers. Next, I wrote about some of my experiences. I was amazed that the other readers wanted to hear these stories. The readers actually pushed me to write this book. To the readers of The Wolverine I thank you. You helped inspire a simple walk- on to put pen to paper and leave his family a memory of one of the greatest experiences imaginable.

I discovered football when I was six years old. There was a new team in the NFL in 1961, a franchise team in Minnesota called the Vikings and I was drawn to an elusive quarterback named Fran Tarkington. As a young boy I dreamed of playing football one day when I was old enough. I didn't think much about the team or the location. Again, I was just a kid with fantasies and dreams.

I followed a few of the NFL teams, particularly the Detroit Lions, Chicago Bears and the Minnesota Vikings. I knew all the players, their numbers, and their records. I played football as much as I could. That was difficult, because as a kid in the suburbs of Detroit it was difficult to get five kids together much less 22 to field an entire team. So I was basically relegated to playing by myself. I would spend hours in the back yard kicking the football straight up into the air and then fielding the ball, imagining that I was the return specialist getting the opening kick off.

By 1967, I was old enough to play Pop Warner and I begged my parents to let me try out for the local team, the Farmington Missiles. Football was in my blood and I did everything an eleven year old kid could do to know, live and breathe the game at that age. I didn't know if it was my future. I wanted it to be, but other than dreams, what can a kid do? The dream took root on November 22, 1969 - the day Bo Schembechler's first Michigan team upset Woody Hayes' best ever Ohio State team-and my life changed forever.

There are a number of people that had influence on that dream. Besides my parents, who were going to support me no matter what I did, the main person that influenced that dream was Bo Schembechler. I was just a kid with a dream, who wanted to pursue that dream with all his heart. Bo was that man that set the stage for that dream to come true. This is our story. This is the story of "Those who stay will be Champions".

CHAPTER 1

THE DREAM

In late November 1969, I was just like most kids in Michigan. I played football in my back yard (mostly by myself) and I'd kick the ball straight up in the air and pretend it was the kick off. I'd catch the ball and dodge imaginary tacklers all the way to the end zone. This would be repeated for hours on end until my mom came out and hollered that it was time for dinner. I'd eat as fast as I could in an effort to get back out to my personal stadium before it got too dark to see the ball.

Tucked in my bed at night, I'd dream of one day donning a helmet and playing for the local high school team, North Farmington. That Saturday I sat down to watch the Michigan vs. Ohio State game. Everyone on the face of the planet knew that Ohio had the greatest team in the last 100 years of football. They had gone undefeated for two years in a row and had crushed Michigan 50-14 the year before, when Woody Hayes made the now famous remark why he went for two after the final score. "Because I couldn't go for three," he had said.

Additionally, Michigan had a brand new coach. Some guy with a name I couldn't even pronounce-"Schembechler." So as a young football fan, I sat down to watch the slaughter. Well, you know what happened. Michigan won 24-12! My life changed that day. I no longer wanted to play for North Farmington. I wanted to play for BO! I wanted to play for Michigan.

My parents heard me proudly profess that one day, I would play for that man and that great school. They sighed as parents do, and told me it was a good quality to follow your dreams. A few hours later, my father shattered those dreams. He announced that the family was moving. We were going to a small town north of San Diego called La Jolla. He had a great job opportunity and we were taking it!

Most kids would jump at the idea of moving to a beach town in California. Not me. I went into a funk. All I could think of was I'd never get to play football (plus I had this huge crush on this cute blond in my 9th grade class. I desperately wanted her to watch me score touchdowns and cheer for me).

It didn't happen. We moved two weeks later into a hotel room on La Jolla Boulevard while we waited to move into our new home. It had a 180 degree view of the Pacific Ocean and was four blocks from the beach. Didn't matter, I was still in a funk. My dad recognized this, and for my Christmas present he said he'd take the family up to see Michigan play in the Rose Bowl. I perked up at that prospect, but again, it was hollow.

When we got to the game, we were informed that Bo had suffered a heart attack and my team went down to defeat to the USC Trojans. I went back into my funk. I decided that I'd never play football and took up beach volleyball instead. Over the next few years I grew some, made a ton of very good friends and discovered that I had an uncanny ability to outrun any and all challengers. Cross country, track; it didn't matter. I'd run the hundred, quarter, half and mile all in the same track meet. Yet I realized that Michigan football was still in my blood when, in my junior year of high school, a buddy asked if I wanted to drive up to Los Angeles to watch Michigan take on UCLA in the Coliseum. When I watched Dennis Franklin and Chuck Heater destroy UCLA that day, my interest in Bo and Michigan sprang up again.

I went home that night and again told my parents that I was going to play football for Michigan. My dad chuckled and asked if I thought it was a good idea to maybe play the sport before I ventured too far. That's when I decided to go out for football my senior year. La Jolla High never really had a good football team. Sure they were great in tennis, golf and surfing, but not football. I had played soccer the year before and decided that I needed a buddy to go out for the team with me. So I asked my friend, Rolf Benirschke. He had the strongest leg on our soccer team so I asked him to be our kicker and I would try out for receiver or safety. Together we decided to play our senior year.

For the first time that decade, La Jolla High had a winning season. I played both safety and split end, having a decent season. I was ready to play for the Michigan Wolverines. So in August 1973, I loaded up my white 1969 mustang with two boxes of clothes and said good-bye to my parents. I had never spoken to Bo, or anyone for that matter at Michigan. I turned left on Nautilus and left again on La Jolla Boulevard to get to Grand Avenue. From there I headed east on interstate 8. I figured 2500 miles in 3 days I'd be in Ann Arbor and tell Bo about my dream to play for Michigan. Piece of cake!

I now embarked on my personal trip. The funk was gone and my good times were about to begin.

CHAPTER 2
MEETING BO

When you're 17 years old and driving alone for 2500 miles, you have some extra time to consider the path you have chosen for yourself. I had a dream. It was a real cool dream. I dreamed that one day I would button up a chinstrap on that beautiful winged helmet and score touchdowns in front of thousands of screaming fans. Reality was over 2000 miles away and it was controlled by a man I'd never met but who had been rumored to cause full-grown men to quiver with fear and stutter when they spoke.

Reality was I had played exactly one year of football at La Jolla High - and did I mention that in reality, I weighed 140 pounds soaking wet? I was wondering if I had done enough to be in shape to play football at Michigan. In shape for what? I had no idea what I was getting myself into. What would I tell Bo? I know - I'd tell him about my dream and the 1969 game. I'd tell him that I had spent all summer on a beautiful sandy beach called Sea Lane playing volleyball. The sand was like sugar, white and coarse, and when you'd jump you would sink down five or six inches and it would absorb all of your power. I knew this would be a great benefit because my knees and ankles were surely battle tested.

Did I say I weighed 140 pounds? All the way through Phoenix to Albuquerque, New Mexico, to Joplin, Missouri, I racked my brain. Was I doing the right thing, what should I expect, how hard could it be? After all I weighed *140 pounds*!

When I pulled into Ann Arbor, I drove straight to my dorm. I had been assigned to a brand new dorm called Markley Hall. It never occurred to me to ask where the football players stayed! So I pulled in, unpacked and inquired as to where was the football building. Some guy said it was part of south campus, but if I was going down to try and get tickets I should have arranged that long before I got to school. School! I hadn't thought about that all the way out here. School was to start on Monday, in two days. The team had been going through double sessions the last two weeks and I didn't even know that!

I was late, so I hurried over to the football office. It was located at 1000 South State Street. I knew I was in the right spot because I saw this long, long brick wall about ten feet high. I ran through the back door and hurriedly asked the receptionist where the football offices were. I got back, "Upstairs". So I bounded the stairs two at a time only to be stopped by another person. She asked what I was doing and in a hurried voice I said, "I'm here to tell Coach Schembechler that I'm here to play for him". She said, "That's great but do you have an appointment?"

I didn't, of course, so I was told to cool my jets and someone else would deal with me. After what seemed like an eternity, a sandy haired little coach came out to talk to me. He invited me into his office and introduced himself as Coach Dennis Brown but everyone called him Denny (my God…I realized this was the guy who was the quarterback of the team when I use to watch them in '67-'68). He was now the freshmen coach. He politely asked what I wanted to do, and I went off again on my dream about the 1969 game and how I fell in love with Michigan.

He stopped me and said Bo would get a kick out of that story but he needed some basics… what school was I enrolled in, when were my classes, where did I play, all the general stuff. He then told me to wait. Ten minutes later I was following him down the hall………to BO's OFFICE! Words probably don't do justice to how I was feeling. The hair on the back of my neck was at attention and my palms were soaking wet. I had a strange feeling that I was just being brought in for amusement.

Bo didn't look up when I entered. He was deep in thought, seemingly reading stats of the final scrimmage. Coach Brown broke the ice by saying, "This kid's got a story for you, Bo". I heard a booming voice say, "OK, let's hear it". I started out nervously about the OSU game in 1969 and when I got to the part about moving to La Jolla he boomed again. "Nothing good ever came outta La Jolla except golfers and surfers, *damn* sure no good football players. You can't weigh more than 140 pounds (How he knew that I'll never know.... my heart sank about 10 feet). What in the world can you offer this team?"

I was mortified and didn't know what to say, but somehow I said I could kick better than anyone he had. After all, I was the second string kicker behind Rolf Benirschke at La Jolla High(but Bo didn't need to know that). So he gave me that much too familiar Bo stare, the one that burns multiple holes through your soul. He finally growled, "Brownie, he can watch practice on Monday and if he still wants to try after that we'll see."

I don't know how it happened but the blood began to flow in my veins again and I felt good. I couldn't wait until Monday.

CHAPTER 3
MY FIRST DAY

My first day with the Wolverines was not like anything I ever expected. Anticipation was the word of the moment for me all day. I don't remember any of my classes or hardly anything else. I do know it must have been a hot day and, as usual, I didn't know what was expected of me. I must have looked like an absolute idiot when I walked past the door that had a sign in big bold letters, "Authorized Personnel Only".

I was wearing cut off jeans (remember this was 1973), no socks, Onistuka Tiger running shoes and a yellow T shirt that had stenciled on the back a picture of a surfer cutting back on a big wave and in blue letters underneath it said, "La Jolla." My heart raced as I walked out on to the tartan practice field and saw the players forming lines for their stretching exercises. Coach Brown passed by me and said, "Go sit over there on those metal bleachers and I'll come by after practice." I did as I was told.

This was a typical Monday game week practice so all the players were in shorts, half shirts and helmets. I swear to you my first thought was, "Damn, these guys aren't all that big." They ran through their drills and I got more and more excited. I was really thinking I might be able to play with these guys.

Formal practice ended and I was all set to tell Coach Brown I was ready for equipment when he came over with another coach. Another short stocky man, who did not look happy (but in real life is one of the greatest guys I've ever known). He was introduced to me as Coach Jerry Hanlon, the special teams coach. Behind him were four guys, Mike Lantry, Bobby Wood and two other guys in street clothes like me. Hanlon said, "OK guys lets see you follow Mike."

They spotted the ball on the 25-yard line on the left hash and Lantry boomed it though the uprights. Bobby Wood also smashed his kick right between the posts and long. Both he and Lantry were straight on toe kickers (Lantry was left footed and Wood right footed). The other two kickers failed miserably and left the competition. My turn came up and I too split the uprights although mine didn't have the height that both Lantry and Wood showed. We moved back to the 30- yard line, then to the 35 and then to the 40, all with similar results. When we lined up from the 45- yard line Lantry went wide left and Wood shanked his kick. Now was my turn. The adrenalin was pumping through me at such a pace I don't think I would have missed from 60 yards out. I crushed the ball and it went farther and higher than anything I had ever kicked in my life and it split the uprights. Wood asked to switch hashes and the same thing happened only I hit that one even better.

As we stopped, Hanlon gave me a smile and said, "Son, can you do that with 11 guys running at you like you stole their dinner." I think I muttered, "Yup" as I was still in amazement that I had made eight field goals in a row. Wood introduced himself and Lantry said hello and we all strolled off the field together. At the door Coach Brown looked at me and said," Nice job, kid, you scared the shit out of them. Let's get you a uniform."

Chapter 4

A Wolverine

Holy cow! I was on the team! I was a Wolverine, but I sure didn't feel like it. I showed up at 2:00pm on Tuesday and was told to get my roll, which was a combination of a half shirt, shorts, jock and socks given to all players. I was then shown to the freshman locker room. Back then it was separated from the Varsity Locker Room, as freshmen had just recently been made eligible to play at the Varsity level. I was given jersey number 26 and I dressed in silence. No one talked to me. Not in the locker room, not on the way to the field and not for the first 30 minutes of practice.

The first 30 minutes consisted of warm ups, kicking, stretching and the specialists (catching passes, punts, kick offs, etc.) Finally, a coach yelled at us to get over to the sidelines. This was where we all stood for the next two hours watching all the other players doing what they were supposed to do. When I say "we" I mean the five or six guys who were kickers that had "no chance" to make the team let alone ever set foot on the turf at Michigan Stadium.

This routine lasted another two days. Then the team went down to play Iowa for the first game in mid September 1973. I listened to the game on the radio as I was as far from making the travel team as you could imagine. Michigan won 31-7 in a relatively routine game. We had a team meeting the following Sunday to review film. This was kind of cool in that we all met as a team in a big room. The offense sat on the left side and the defense sat on the right side of the room facing Bo. As a kicker, it didn't matter where I sat as long as it wasn't in the first 10 rows of the 11 row room. It was very evident that walk-ons and kickers were subject to the last row and we had to be very respectful of upperclassmen.

I didn't know this at the time, but when I was driving the 2500 miles to get to Ann Arbor the team was in double sessions. During that time two of the eight wide receivers had been lost to injury. I also didn't know that the reason two of the eight receivers went down were because of Don Dufek and Dave Brown. These Michigan All- American defensive backs had trashed those guys. So by shear numbers the offense needed six receivers to play for the first three teams, so during the 5th practice that I attended, when Don Dufek hit Jerry Collins and he left the practice field the defensive back coach, Jack Harbaugh, ran over to the sidelines where we were all standing and asked," Have any of you ever played wide receiver before?"

Before anyone could blink my hand shot up (Heaven knows why I did this – I *still* don't know). Maybe it was my love for the game; maybe it was my love for Michigan. Jack grabbed me and told me that I was his "new" scout team receiver. The scout team was the group that was supposed to act as if they were the team that Michigan was playing that week, so this meant I was supposed to be a Stanford receiver for the week.

Since I didn't know the first thing to do, I ran to the huddle and lined up in back. The graduate assistant coach held up a diagram that showed the next play that we were supposed to run against the first string defense. It was a straight, drop back pass where the wide receiver ran a 13- yard hook route. I lined up and ran my pattern. The ball sailed over my head by 10 feet. I didn't even jump because it was so far over my head.

Didn't matter, Dave Brown ran through me like a ton of bricks! He hit me so hard I thought I was going to lose the fillings in my teeth. Then, the damndest thing happened. He picked me up, as if to help me, but at the same time he yelled, "Go for the ball rookie." Somehow I gathered myself and ran back to the huddle."Holy sh--, what have I gotten myself into here?"

I was intimidated, scared out of my mind and had zero friends that I could talk with, but somehow I lined up for the next play and the next and the next. After practice I showered in silence, got dressed and hopped on my bicycle back to Markley Hall (where I had missed dinner). They had a snack shop in the basement that was open after hours. So I went down there and ordered my first dorm pizza. I think it was at this time that I also decided that I could not survive at 140 pounds. So after the pizza, I ordered a chocolate ice cream sundae and I began the most incredible journey of my life.

If you only knew what was going through my head. It was as far away from anything related to having a good time as can be humanly possible.

Chapter 5

My Nickname

We've all heard the Charles Dickens quote, "It was the best of times, it was the worst of times." That pretty much summed up the first few days at Michigan.

My dream had become a reality. I had confronted Bo and he had given me a shot. I had astonished myself by kicking so well (without pads on) and the coaches were duly impressed. I stood around for a few days then fate through me into the breech on the scout team. I had been "drilled" on more than one occasion to the point where I thought I might not be able to get up, but somehow I did. I promised myself that I would eat a pizza and a hot fudge sundae every night until I weighed a respectable 185 pounds.

Every day I gave it my all, and still no one talked to me (other than a coach yelling at me to do something). Bo hadn't acknowledged my existence since the day I was in his office. I didn't hold that against him. He was always on the other side of the field with the offense. You might think that one would start to get confused about their lot in life and where they were headed but, that never happed. That dream to run out on to Michigan's field kept pushing me every day. I had to get bigger, faster, better, every day, every time out on the practice field.

Sure, I was lonely. There were no football players living in my dorm and I rode my bike to and from practice alone and in silence. I hadn't bothered to call my parents to tell them what was going on because I really didn't have much to say. I was practice meat and that was it. As I mentioned, my dorm's kitchen was closed by the time I got back from practice, but there was a sweet elderly lady named Alice that hid a tray full of food in the far side of the kitchen, and she always left the side door open. Every night she'd fill that tray for me, and every time I saw her at lunch I thanked her.

That was the only relationship I had for the first month of school. As I wrote, it was both the best of times and the worst of times. I loved what I was doing, but I had no one to share it with... not that anyone would have given much thought about a football walk-on, anyway. But I did have Alice, many times she'd put two or three desserts on the tray because she knew I was trying to gain weight and make the team. She was such a sweet lady. Wherever you are Alice, thank you.

One of the unique things that impacted a scout team player back then was the fact that Michigan's defense was so good that most of the teams that played Michigan threw the ball rather than try and run it down their throats. So, if you were a scout team receiver and you were emulating the opposing players you were going to run a lot of passing plays against some very good defensive backs.

Through all of this, I had three things going for me. Two of these qualities came from hard work and persistence. I was fast and could run all day long, so running 60-70 pass patterns over the course of a practice was not difficult to do. I also had good hands. I'm not sure if this came from all the years of playing volleyball or the thousands of passes my high school buddy used to throw to me, but I could catch the ball.

The third quality came from good heredity. I was blessed with a relatively high threshold to accept pain. I think this came from my mom's side, but somehow this was passed down to me. When you mix that together with a system that throws the ball a lot I was in a perfect environment to succeed and maybe- just maybe- I wanted it more than some other people. It had never occurred to me to complain about the heat, the cold, the bruises, the coaches or the myriad of things I heard from some of the other guys.

Why bother? That wasn't going to help the Wolverines; *my* Wolverines win the next game. So I continued to go out there and run slants against Don Dufek, who would explode into me and shake his head as I got up every time and made it back to the huddle. Every now and then I'd break free and make a circus catch only to be drilled twice as hard the next time a ball came my way (presumably because we had made the defense look bad.)

After a few weeks we were told by Coach Brown that the reserves were going to play the Notre Dame reserves. To get ready for this, after the next practice all the freshmen, walk-ons and non- traveling upperclassmen were going to have a scrimmage. All of us got really excited. This was going to be the first time without starters that we were going to be able to show the coaches what we could accomplish.

On Wednesday before the team was to travel to play MSU in East Lansing the reserves scheduled a scrimmage. Like so many other aspects walk-ons were delegated to be subservient to upperclassmen. The two receivers getting most of the reps were Jerry Collins and Doug MacKenzie (a sophomore and junior respectively). Doug, whether it was because he felt sorry for me or because he was melancholy because he wasn't traveling motioned for me to go in for him and take his place.

These scrimmages were fairly unorganized with a lot of different guys getting a lot of different looks. What I do remember was we ran a "sally" and I was on the opposite side of the field. The play was Bo's reverse and I ran across the whole field to see if I could get a block in. A freshman defensive end named Eric Phelps was chasing down the play from the backside and had no idea where I was or where I was coming from. This was a blind but clean shot and I decleated him right at the sidelines right in front of the coaches.

The entire sideline went into an uproar as we all loved to see big hits. As he got up Eric said," Where the hell did you come from?" All I could muster at the time was, "I came from La Jolla!" That was the first time a scholarship player had spoken to me in five weeks. After this, I earned a nickname, which is sort of a right of passage on the team. From here on I was known as "Surf".

CHAPTER 6

BO KNOWS

Now I was known as "Surf", mostly because I was from La Jolla and probably because no one else had anything on me. Over the years there were hundreds of names that wouldn't have any significance to anyone other than your teammates. To us, they were our brands, our rights of passage.

The names flowed easily back then, "Z", Big Fella, Surf, "T", Beef, Flame, Kid, Paw, Zoo, Huck even Pumkinhead and Molester (no, don't bother to ask – his anonymity is safe with me).

The other right of passage was to actually get on the field. That was pretty far off for me, but what was coming up was our reserve game against Notre Dame. The varsity went off to play MSU in East Lansing, so we were free to go down to South Bend and play the Irish scout team on Friday. What was so weird about these games was everything was foreign to just about everyone.

An example. The coaches were now tasked with running the Michigan offense and the Michigan defense, with players that had been running scout team offenses and defenses since the end of double sessions. We were supposed to know the plays that we hadn't run in over six weeks and as freshmen we barely knew them anyway. Add the fact that we were also playing with guys in positions that they had never played before and it was an all out debacle.

Standout running back Rob Lytle and receiver Jim Smith for example, were freshmen, but they were on the travel squad, so we had no tailback or receiver (unless these positions were played by an upperclassman). The upper classmen were never really into these games as it meant they *weren't* on the travel team. We had linebackers playing fullback and tackles playing tight end. It was obvious that Notre Dame was going through the same problems and soon the game morphed into a free- for-all with everyone caring only about physical punishment and "big hits".

If I recall, we fumbled inside our own 10- yard line and allowed them an easy score. Then they fumbled inside *their* own ten yard line and *we* had an easy score. Then we threw an interception that they ran back for a score and it ended mercifully, 14-7. I didn't get in one play and was relegated to spectator the whole game. Fortunately, our sour taste was washed away the next day when the Varsity beat MSU 31-0 with Dave Brown running back a punt for a touchdown in that one to keep them undefeated.

Two weeks later, we went down to play Toledo reserves, and it got even worse. I did get to start the game as they put me in as the kicker and I shanked the opening kick off about thirty yards that took about twenty crazy hops and pinned them inside their ten- yard line.

This game was just as bad as our last reserve game. There were turnovers and mistakes, and we were down by 14 starting the second half. Coach Brown told us at half time that no Michigan reserve team had ever lost to Toledo and he damn sure wasn't going to be the first coach to that happen. To prove it, he told us he was scrapping the offense and we were going to do what we all practiced all the time… passing the ball. Trouble was that as a scout team the coaches held up diagrams that showed which patterns we should run. Besides the Michigan offense really only had play action passes, and we really didn't know half of them.

So in the second half our offense went like this: Jerry Zuver was installed at quarterback (yep, the guy who ended up as a wolfman later). Zuv would make up a play in the huddle that went like this, "Line you block, J you run deep, Surf you cut behind him at fifteen over the middle. On one." We ran the play to perfection except Zuv threw a wounded duck that the linebacker tipped. As luck would have it, the tip came right to me and I picked up thirty five yards.

Two more passes and we were inside the 10- yard line, but we fumbled. At the end of the day I had four catches for one hundred yards and Zuv ran for a 75 yard touchdown late in the game but it wasn't enough. We lost by the same 14-7 score.

At the Sunday team meeting, Bo excused everyone except the guys that played in the reserve game. As he read off the stats, he grew madder and madder. Finally, he hollered, "You sons a bitches are the worst group I ever brought into Michigan. You don't deserve to play on this field and wear this uniform and I highly doubt any of you ever will get the chance." Then he turned to his coaches and told them that Michigan would never, ever play a reserve game again.

I'm not sure if they ever have. All I know is that we never played another one the next four years I was there. Bo stormed out of the room. As everyone else sat in stunned silence, Coach Brown told me that Bo wanted to see me. He said to run out to the parking lot and catch him at his car.

When I got to within 10 feet he said," Brownie told me that you and Zuver were our only players down there......I got an eye on you kid." He got in his car and drove away. This was the second time in my life Bo acknowledged my existence and I was on top of the world.

CHAPTER 7
1973 OHIO STATE

Saturday, November 24, 1973 was the first day that I actually got to put on a Michigan game jersey and pants. I had practiced every day since early September and never saw the inside of the Michigan locker room at the Big House. Finally, it happened. It was Ohio State week, and Bo wanted as many Wolverines on the field as possible. We were going to be over 115 strong and as such had several players with identical numbers.

This was also my first time for a lot of things. The first time running down the tunnel. The first time on the tartan field. The first time in front of 105,000 fans. The first time on TV. It was damn near my first time for everything. Even though I had about as much chance of playing as the man in the moon it didn't matter. I had so much adrenalin flowing through me that I floated across the field. The passes in warm ups seemed like they were in slow motion. Everything was so alive, so keen, so distinct, so vibrant. I wanted this feeling to last forever.

It was not the prettiest day, overcast and damp. I didn't notice. I had turned 18 three weeks before and had been dreaming of this day for four straight years. We were going to win and I would be going to the Rose Bowl. No one from La Jolla would believe it. Not my high school buddies, not my teachers, not my parents. Half of me was thinking. "Damn, dreams really do come true. You deserve this, Curt; you've worked so hard and overcome so much."

The other half was still dreaming, "What would it be like if you got the chance to play and scored the winning touchdown." Well, all of that changed as soon as the game started. This was a good old fashioned smash mouth football game, going back and forth. Michigan seemed to have the momentum and was definitely dominating in yardage and first downs. There were a lot of people in the stands whose stomachs were in knots, so imagine how all the poor players like me who couldn't do anything to impact the game were feeling.

Even with momentum on Michigan's side Ohio State scored first. Then being down 10-0 at halftime Michigan fought back to tie the game with only a few minutes remaining. The Michigan defense shut down the Buckeyes and got the ball back for one last push. Finally when they stopped Mike Lantry lined up for a 58- yard field goal. He hit it solidly, but it was just wide to the left. My heart sank. The Buckeyes took over on the 20 yard line. The next two minutes were amazing. For one, they actually attempted a pass. One of the guys that I had run patterns against all year, Tom Drake, intercepted giving Michigan one last field goal attempt. I was standing on the metal bench and jumped so high I missed the bench on the way down. After crashing to the turf, I was surrounded by fifteen other freshmen who had also been standing on the bench. I realized I hadn't missed the bench; it had fallen over from the weight of all of the guys.

By that time, the place was rocking. I had to get a better look, so I went as far as I could to the opposite end of the bench (the south end). I was standing on the southern tip of the 30- yard line and I was in great position to see the 33- yard field goal attempt of Mike Lantry. He hit it true. I know the referee said it was wide left, and others have said it went right over the post. All I can tell you is what I saw. Mike had hit it so high that it was at least twenty feet above where the post stopped. From my angle, I thought it was about a foot inside the left upright. He was kicking from the right hash, so the flight of the ball took it to the left after it passed above the posts.

I thought he made it and I jumped up and down as I thought I was going to Pasadena. The one official on the right side made no motion at all, and he looked to the guy on the other side. That official signaled that it was wide. I stood there stunned for some time. I couldn't imagine how Mike felt. The game ended in a strange 10-10 tie.

In the locker room we found out that Dennis Franklin, had broken his collar bone. All that said we were still Big Ten Champs.

We had played the number 1 team in the country straight up and really should have won the game. Surely we were going to get the nod to go to Pasadena.

CHAPTER 8

INJUSTICE

In the hours following the game, Big Ten country was ablaze with rumor. The radio shows couldn't get the proper protocol for picking the Rose Bowl representative. I didn't know the process myself, but we were all sure we were going to be picked. I can't remember sleeping that night, but I know I wasn't tired the next day as we all funneled into the meeting room.

We all came to attention as Bo entered the room. He started to say something about "the worst injustice he's ever known" and I didn't hear the rest. I was shattered. I could see rage in his eyes but I couldn't hear what he was saying. My mind was both racing and frozen at the same time. Bo was literally shaking as he pounded the podium. Somehow, I heard that we lost a vote and the reason why was our starting quarterback wouldn't be able to play in the Rose Bowl and they (who are "they" I wondered?) wanted the best representative.

I remember thinking. "What about the other 114 guys who worked their butts off to go undefeated? They can play in the game." We were all in a fog. We needed answers to so many questions. Hadn't we showed the resolve to come back from a 10- point deficit? Weren't we the ones with the ball at the end of the game with the chance to win? We had more first downs, more yardage- damn it, we were the better team.

This was perhaps the most bitter pill that any Wolverine has ever had to swallow. We didn't lose. We weren't cheated by a clock malfunction or a bad call or trickery or anything that happened on the field. Our legs had been cut out from under us by some outside athletic directors. Most of who didn't even watch the game.

Franklin's collarbone healed quickly, and he was even throwing footballs by Christmas. Every Michigan fan has heard this story, but I was there, and to this day, it still hurts. I was going home to California for the New Year, but not the way I wanted. Bo would tell us that we get strong through adversity, so that day I made a new resolution to myself. I had dreamed of playing for Michigan one day. I worked hard, persisted and improved. Now, I had to leave no doubt in anyone's mind that I deserved to be on the field, because this could never happen again.… not to me, not to Michigan.

I know a number of my teammates felt the same way. The 1974 season was going to be the year that this all came together. Good times were going to roll.

CHAPTER 9

NEW RESOLVE

When the shock from the Rose Bowl snub subsided, two things happened. First, as I've mentioned before, I developed a burning desire to cut my own path and never, ever allow an injustice like that to happen again. I think Bo felt the same because, he went on such a war path telling who ever would listen that he had a team that had gone 20-1-1 the last two years and was sitting at home while other teams with four losses in one year were playing in bowl games.

My respect for Bo was already great, but that was revolving around him being a football coach. Now he was a man on a mission to right a wrong and change the way the Big Ten functioned forever. He was set on changing college football.

The second thing that happened was understandable. I went into a funk. I had never been as high in my life as I was when I ran on to that field on November 24, 1973, and that was stripped away. The next thing I knew the season is over. All the guys packed up and went home for Thanksgiving. There was no way I was going to get on a plane to fly back home for three to four lousy days with everyone who knew me either asking silly questions or giving me a hard time. I wanted none of that.

It was fitting when the Resident Assistant at Markley Hall came around late Wednesday and said the dorm was being closed for the holiday. There would be no food service, and everyone was to leave. In my state of mind I was in, I did what I thought was best for me. I told him I was going to go to a friend's house. Because I lived in Markley I didn't hang with football players. They all lived in West Quad. Most of them took off early anyway.

So there I sat all alone in a dorm that normally housed about 1600 students, without food service, to boot. It really hit home when I decided to call home on Thursday, Thanksgiving Day, and my mom asked me where I was going to have my turkey. I told her that I was eating a tuna sandwich and that was good enough. She began to cry.

I was already in a downer mood and that certainly didn't help, so I holed myself up and told myself there will be better days and better times ahead.

Yep, Bo had always told us we get stronger through adversity. Well, right about then I was feeling like I was pinned down by a thousand-pound rock. If I believed in Bo, if I believed in Michigan, if I truly thought that "Those who stay will be Champions" then I would have to get stronger.

That would be my resolution for the next year… adversity will make you stronger. If I stayed, I would be a champion.

CHAPTER 10
WINTER CONDITIONING

In the 1970's, winter conditioning wasn't even close to what the team does today. We didn't have Schembechler Hall and the indoor facility they have today. The early part of 1974 the Michigan Football team still used a Universal Gym (one) with six- to- eight stations. So lifting weights really wasn't an option.

This was our typical work out during winter conditioning. We'd all get dressed in the locker room at the practice facility on State Street. Then we'd walk over to Crisler Arena. The coaches would then break us up into position groups, with receivers and defensive backs in one group, offensive line and defensive line in another group and the running backs and linebackers would be in a third. The kickers just joined in wherever.

Then we'd have three stations. The first station was running laps around the concourse of the arena. Sometimes we would do long distance running (20 laps). Other times we'd do sprints. This was usually hysterical because you'd have 20-30 guys in a group going full speed on curved parts of the concourse. I can assure you this "track" was not designed for 220- pound men running full tilt. There were some of the most hilarious pile- ups this side of NASCAR and we were all in tennis shoes that were, by design, not meant to be used in the fashion we were using them.

The next station was the wrestling mats down in the basement. We couldn't use the floor because Johnny Orr's basketball team was practicing there. On the mats we'd do agility drills like "monkey rolls", up downs, and lunges. Then we'd spend some time on cone drills with zigzags, four corners, cut backs and all kinds of crazy stuff.

From there we would head to the last station, which was the stairs. We'd run these, and then hop (both feet, single right, single left), then we'd hop some more, skipping every other step and this would continue until your legs were burning. On decent days outside we'd run the golf course, which everyone hated (and by "decent day" I mean it wasn't snowing). That meant that if it was 10 degrees and not snowing we'd run outside. I can't tell you how many times I ran that course when the temperature was below freezing and when you came indoors and breathed in the warm air it seemed to serrate your lungs.

Even here, freshmen were not allowed to pass a senior and walk-ons weren't even up to the level of freshmen, so I stayed in the middle of the pack the first few times even though I knew I could run faster. Every now and then when we went outside I'd burst by some upperclassman and get yelled at (in my defense, I was just trying to stay warm). Dave Brown was the first to put me in my place. He'd say something that was a half growl along the lines of, "Get to the back, rookie."

But I had spent the entire season of 1973 waggling behind these upperclassmen and I wasn't about to do that again. Plus, Brown was the guy who was encouraging me everyday in practice to go harder at him to "give him a good look". He always wanted our best shot. He made sure we knew that if he didn't get better neither would we and the whole team would suffer.

Dave Brown was a true disciple of Bo and a true leader. He always insisted you played like you practiced and you practiced like you played –always 100 percent effort. I'm not sure if it was the fire in my belly over being cheated out of the Rose Bowl, Dave Brown pushing me, or my need to prove myself to Bo and the team but I decided not to hold back.

The next time we went to run at Crisler I was determined to break out. When the defensive backs and receivers lined up for a distance run Brown was in front and I started about 20 guys behind him. We started out at a good clip, and it was tough to pass guys because we were basically running in a big circle. After a few laps I had passed everyone but Brown. I knew if I was going to do this it would have to be dramatic, so right when we got to the end of the next lap, right in front of the coaches I hit it full throttle.

I went by him in a flash and heard one of the coaches' say, "Damn". I poured it on and didn't slow down even when I was lapping guys. When I finished, Jack Harbaugh looked at me and said, "Son, I knew you could run but I've never seen anything like that before. You're going to have to keep that up 'cause I don't want to see what happens if Brown ever catches you!"

From that day on I never lost a race at Michigan. Even the great Dave Brown never caught me.

CHAPTER 11

BACK HOME

I left Ann Arbor in late April 1974 for my second cross-country drive. This time I was going back to California.

A number of things happened the previous year. I gained 40 pounds and surprisingly got faster. My confidence was high because I had taken the best shots that the best players from the University of Michigan had to offer. The team had gone 10-0-1 and was considered one of the best teams in the land, but we had not gone to a bowl game and as a result I had resolved to come back bigger, faster, and stronger than the year before.

How I was going to accomplish this being 2500 miles from Ann Arbor was a mystery to me, but hey, I was 18 years old and had the world by the tail. So, the trusty white mustang was loaded up with all of my belongings, and I headed west on Hwy 94. I must say I missed the warm days and the ocean breeze.

By mid- day of my second day on the road, I stopped in Fort Worth, Texas. The reason for that detour was to see my high school girlfriend at TCU. We had had a standard high school relationship (she was the head cheerleader and I was the track star and captain of the football team).

As I've previously mentioned I didn't play football until my senior year. Partly was because she wanted me to concentrate on track and to do that I had to run cross-country in the fall instead of playing football.

That all changed my senior year when, if I was to make good on my promise to myself and my parents that I'd play for Michigan one day, I decided that I'd better go out for the football team.

Over the past nine months, each of us had changed dramatically. She now looked different (as did I). She couldn't believe how much bigger I was, and I couldn't believe how dark her hair had grown, it was no longer bleached by the California sun.

It was a nice visit but short. There was a nice surprise as a buddy of mine from high school flew out to Fort Worth and said he'd drive back to San Diego with me. His name was Bookie Treloar. He had thrown over 200 passes a day to me all last summer getting me ready for my try out at Michigan.

That morning, we headed west again. After 3 hours of me driving, we switched and he got behind the wheel. Within two miles, he was pulled over for speeding and it was a scene right out of the movies. The patrolman asked for all the particulars and told Bookie he had clocked him at 77 when the limit was 70. Since we were from out of state he told us we had to go before the judge that afternoon and we needed to follow him into the town.

We were just outside Odessa, Texas. After a quick hearing, Book was assessed a $20 fine (remember this was 1974). We figured the patrolman and the judge headed for the bar with our money. Book was so pissed he didn't drive again until mid way through New Mexico. This time he got five miles before being pulled over, *again*. Man, he had bad luck. He didn't drive the rest of the way home.

Once home, I quickly got into a routine. At 8:00 am I would run between five and seven miles. I had logged over 900 in 90 days the summer before and my goal was to do 800 in 100 days (after all I was 40 pounds heavier). Around 10:00 am I'd hit Sea Lane. This was the sandy white beach I had learned to play volleyball on in high school. My teacher was a La Jolla legend (I'm not kidding here). His name was Jack Macpherson.

If you ever read the book by Tom Wolfe, The Pump House Gang, you'd know Jack. He was the self appointed Chairman of Mac Meda. The book is about the 60's beach life style and an underground society, called Mac Meda Destruction Company. It was all made up stuff that just allowed these guys to drink beer, and have fun but Jack was the "Mac" of Mac Meda.

By the time I met him, Jack was absorbed in beach volleyball and taught me how to play. I'd play every day until about 5:00 pm. Then I'd head up to La Jolla High School and run a few more miles. Book would show up around 5:15 to 5:30 and start to throw me passes…. 10 at my chest, 10 at my right shoulder, 10 at my left shoulder, 10 at my waist, 10 at each knee and 10 at each ankle. Then we'd start over, but I'd be turned sideways.

Once I did both sides, we start over again and we do all of the same one handed, first the right hand then the left and when we finished this that's when we start running patterns. Again, it was pretty boring to anyone not intending on playing college football. I'd do 10 outs to the right, then to the left, 10 slants, 10 hooks, 10 corners, 10 posts, and 10 flies all each way, right and left. If there was someone to run against we'd do that, too.

By 6:30 pm we'd stop for dinner. The last thing we did was Book would stand 10 yards away and he'd wing the ball at me as hard as he could. After each catch I'd take a step closer and repeat until I was only a few feet away. We usually fell down laughing because at two feet I couldn't catch anything (plus he stopped throwing as hard)! We'd both rush home for dinner and then it was to the La Jolla Recreation Center to play basketball until 9:00 pm. The next morning I'd start the day all over again. As I said, there was no way that anyone would be able to claim I wasn't in better shape than I had been the year before.

I was bound and determined that by August 1974 I'd be in better condition than anyone else on the team. This was going to be my time to shine. I had "stayed" and Michigan was crowned "Champions" but it was hallow. I burned for the real thing. I wanted to be considered part of the team and earn a championship ring on my own. Bo and the whole team were going to see that this kid from California deserved to be a Wolverine.

I dreamed at night that this would be my destiny.

CHAPTER 12

BOOKIE

I've talked about my friend, Bookie, and how he helped me in my effort to try out for the Michigan Football team. He also was a tremendous help in my efforts to stay in shape over the years I played at Michigan. I owe him a lot in this regard, and since I'm sharing stories with you about Michigan I have to share a Bookie story.

Book made me laugh, every day. He was as unusual a character as anyone I had ever met. He was a world class practical joker. Just about every day in high school, walking in the hall, he would reach around who ever he was walking with and pinch a girl on the other side. He'd immediately spin and look at the wall as if he was totally oblivious as to what just happened. The end result was one of the guys he was walking with would usually get accused of the pinching crime and either get slapped or made fun of by everyone.

Another standard operation for him would be to get someone to look away (there were hundreds of variations on this) at the lunch table. At just the right moment he would steal and eat whatever he wanted off their plate. It was absolutely childish, silly and hilarious. None of this was ever done with intent to hurt anyone, only to get laughs. Bookie always wanted everyone to like him and laugh at him. He once worked at an ice cream parlor and would always give his "buddies" (I think this was everyone) extra scoops of ice cream.

When he was uncovered and immediately dismissed, somehow-no one knows how- he walked out of the place with a five gallon drum of cookies and cream.

Bookie had some of the fastest hands around, and we would play those silly hand slap games for hours until our hands were numb with pain, but we'd laugh our heads off in the process. Down at the beach, Sea Lane, you really needed to be on your toes. If you weren't you would be "pantsed" at the absolute worst moment possible. The result here would be hundreds of beach goers busting their stitches watching a bare assed guy chase Bookie around the beach.

One of the most important things to Bookie (besides keeping the school in stitches) was to get into a football game. He wasn't a very good football player and didn't get into any games. He always used to boast, "I'll make history if I ever get in a game." We used to just take that as another "Bookie-ism". Finally, after a few injuries and in a blow out game he got his opportunity. He was a middle guard on the defense. I was playing safety so I was right behind him by 10 yards.

When he came to the huddle he announced, "Watch me." I had no idea what he was up to but I wasn't going to miss this for anything. When the center came up and got over the ball Bookie got out of his stance, turned and winked at me. He then got back in his stance and immediately sent the center ass over elbows with a forearm shiver. Out comes the yellow hanky. Fifteen yards, unsportsmanlike conduct. I started to laugh when Bookie put his hands on his head as if to say, "Oh my god, what a bonehead move, what did I just do?

The referee marched off the fifteen yards and we lined up again. As soon as the center came out again, Book turned and winked again. I know I yelled, "Don't do it" and started to run towards the center but I was too late. Sure enough, "BAM"- another shiver to the head. A minor melee broke out, but after order was restored our coach pulled him from the game and he never played again.

As he was pulled off the field by the coach, he smiled and looked back at the huddle. It was foolish and crazy, for sure, but nobody got hurt and I didn't stop laughing until the fourth quarter.

Football brings out all kinds. No matter how you look at it, those were good times with fun people.

CHAPTER 13
DOUBLES 1974

My third cross country trip originated in late July 1974 and it seemed as though I could finally make it without a map. I was actually getting pretty good at driving long distances.

I wanted to get to Michigan early for many reasons. I had missed double sessions in '73 because I didn't know any better. This time I wanted to be there from the get go. I also wanted to visit my grandparents, who were getting up there in age and I didn't know how much more time I would have with them. Besides, my grandfather had been accomplished soccer player in Scotland and he adored sports, so we had a lot in common.

More than anything, I couldn't wait to prove myself. That horrible feeling of the OSU tie and sitting at home when others were playing in bowl games was burning through me. That feeling had gnawed at me all summer, and there was a huge desire to do something about it. So three and a half days later I pulled into Detroit (my 1969 mustang really performed well). I parked on Prest Street, where my grandparents had a modest home. We talked and laughed, and I told them how everyone in the family was doing fine. I ate like a king as my Grandmother's cooking ability was unmatched.

The next day I painted their garage and knocked off around 6pm so I could go for a long run. The following day I cleaned out all of their rain gutters and re-caulked all the roof penetrations. Grandpa wanted to pay me, but there was no way I could take any money from him. They were feeding me after all.

That afternoon I went to a park right next to Mercy Hospital and ran repeat 40- yard dashes until I dropped. Then the next morning I drove to Ann Arbor to report for my first double sessions, but my second season as a Wolverine. We were all given rooms in South Quad, and the typical chatter abounded as the new freshmen checked in.

Bo had done an amazing job bringing in some high profile athletes. The list was pretty impressive. There was a group of big linemen with some good credentials like Bill Dufek, Walt Downing, Mark Donohue and a tall skinny kid named Mike Kenn. There were some tough linebackers named John Anderson and Dominic Tedesco and an all-Chicago running back named Kevin King. Bo also landed some pretty good skill guys as defensive backs named, Dwight Hicks, Jim Pickens and Derek Howard.

Yet, the cream of the crop were the running backs, Dennis Richardson, Max Richardson and a big fullback named Scotty Corbin out of Cincinnati.

Bo had brought in only one receiver, who was a skinny kid much smaller than me from somewhere in Ohio, Andy Jackson., as all of the receivers were undergraduates in 1973.

The coaching staff annually handed out the "Best Conditioned Athlete" award after the first few days of camp. We'd run the mile, repeat 40- yard dashes, and other stuff that was the basis for this award. In future years this became a point- based award which we were awarded points based upon times, amount lifted or repetitions. But in 1974 it was more of a coach's judgment call.

On the second day I shattered the team record for the mile and no one knew what to do about it. So that night at the team meeting, Bob Thornblaugh, who was a Graduate Assistant, presented me a plaque for the record, but only after they gave the best conditioned athlete to Geoff Steger. There was comfort from the fact that I was already turning some heads and we had a great group of young players from which to build Michigan's future.

I kept repeating to myself, "Those who stay will be champions." I had to show all that I could withstand the pressures and succeed. This was to be the time of my life.

CHAPTER 14

A FULL RIDE

I was living a dream, a California kid walking on to the University of Michigan Football Team. I had showed up at Bo's office and he gave me a chance. Imagine the hair on the back of your neck when you're 17 years old, 6' 1", 140 lbs and you're looking into Bo's eyes and he growls at you that " nothing good ever came outta La Jolla except golfers, tennis players and surfers." He relented and told me I could watch a practice. It took a few weeks to get into a scrimmage and after that I was the leading "scout" team receiver on the team. By the end of the '73 season I was still 6'1" but now a respectable 180 lbs. I never got into a game and in my gut it seemed I wasn't really part of the team until I saw game action. You can call it crazy because I was contributing on the scout team, but when your buddies from high school don't see you play and you don't suit up for games, it's really hard to swallow.

But 1974 was going to be my year to finally get into a game. I dressed out for the opener, but didn't get into the game. There are few things in life that can compare to running down the tunnel at the Big House and crossing the field to touch the banner, so I was on cloud 9. For the Colorado game, I also dressed. We were in pregame formation, stretching, when Bo came up to me and delivered a message that would forever change my life. He said, "Curt, we're going to redshirt you, so that means you won't play this year at all, but I'm giving you a full grant."

A full grant meant instant credibility with the rest of the team. In 1973 I had come in with 33 guys, all of whom were either all-state, or all- conference while some were All- Americans. There were eight walk-ons and all of them were at a minimum, all-league, except me. I called my parents to give them the news and they were excited for me. Actually, it was a huge blessing, as my father had just started his own company and he wasn't sure that he could afford out of state tuition, something I didn't find out about until a few years later.

Later that season I received a package in my locker. It was the 1973 Big Ten Championship ring. Now, I knew I was part of the team. This was one of the greatest moments of my early Michigan career. This is a special ring for those of you who know your Michigan Football history. Every Championship ring has your name and other significant info engraved on the sides. If you played in the Rose Bowl either the score or the words "Rose Bowl" is printed on the sides. The 1973 rings are blank. Bo did this on purpose. We had tied OSU 10-10 and five athletic directors of the other Big Ten universities voted for Ohio State to go to the Rose Bowl. Bo wanted to remind all of us of that crime committed against Michigan football players.

As I looked at my ring, I knew and felt I was part of something special, and it was great. I was now a Michigan Football player.

CHAPTER 15

BACK WOODS

Yes, Michigan football was quite different back in 1974, yet at the time there were some things that seemed strangely similar to today. Looking back now, I can see patterns in how Bo recruited. I was a bigger, faster version of Keith Johnson who started at split end before me. I even tried to emulate Keith in practice and I will tell all he was a fine mentor. Running back Rob Lytle was a bigger, faster version of former running back Chuck Heater.

You could see these patterns at almost all the positions and with good reason. We were an option team, built on speed and quickness on both sides of the ball.

The other great thing about Michigan football is that you get to meet the greatest guys in the world from all over the country. That's truly a place where differences show up and personalities collide. My freshman year Bo, recruited a clone of Larry Gustafson, who played from 1971 through 1973 at wingback. Larry was about 5'9', 180 pounds, was fast enough, had decent hands and had a perfect attitude, willing to stick his nose in the fight and mix it up. Gus's clone was a guy by the name of Daryl Truitt. He was a bigger, faster version of Gus, plus he had brownish curly hair just like Gus.

Daryl was from Kentucky and has an easygoing manner similar to Gus an unassuming, very likeable guy. Gus remained on as a graduate assistant coach in 1974 and tried to mentor Daryl at the wing back position, but try as he might he just couldn't get Daryl to take it to the next level. It soon became clear that Daryl was out of his element. Big time football, big university, and difficult classes all took a toll on him.

Even through all of this we all loved hanging around with him. We had a pretty unique crew that hung out freshman year. Picture this: me from California talking about beaches, babes and bodysurfing, Daryl talking about hunting in the back woods of Kentucky, Eric Phelps, from New Hampshire talking about skiing and the east coast's "better beer". We were having blast.

One of my fondest memories will prove how times were different back then, when the drinking age was 18 years old. While on the third floor of West Quad, windows open, drinking beer, listening to The Who's Quadraphenia on the record player – something I'll never forget. Daryl hands each of us a plate of small stringy meat that he's been grilling over a hot plate. With his Kentucky drawl he says that it's squirrel.

Yep, one of the fluffy tailed one from across the street. He claimed to have shot it with his .22 rifle, skinned it and was proud to be serving it to his buddies. I really didn't care if he was joking or not. I loved being part of this group and loved being part of Michigan football.

CHAPTER 16
BRAIN WAVES

When you're involved in a big time program like Michigan, there are always extracurricular things happening. Some of these revolve around being some sort of guinea pig. There are always companies wanting to test new products like painkillers, ointments, treatments, pads, and equipment, whatever someone thinks they can make money on and who better to have an endorsement than the Michigan Wolverines?

In 1974 the Michigan football program decided that they would engage in a month long test on helmets. The program was to test McGregor, Bike, and Rawlings helmets. From 1970 through 1974, all Michigan players wore McGregor helmets. At the end of double sessions that season a group of "test" players were selected to wear the other kind of helmets. I was one of those to be tested.

There wasn't any science in the method that was used to select the players. Bo told the company that they could use any walk-on or red shirt player they wanted because none of these guys were going to get into a game anyway. His rationale was that by using these guys there was no way it could negatively impact the team. I mean, come on, if some guy who was never going to play cracked his skull it wouldn't have been all that big of a deal.

Bo wasn't being callous-- just practical. While all of the "regular" players wore the famous "winged" helmet the "test" guys ran around in these "sea blue" plain helmets. The first part of the test was the most bizarre and I learned a lot. They had doctors who were going to track various levels of brain activity before, during and after practice all month long.

Then after the season, some players had to be retested to make sure that everything was back to normal. To get a good read each guinea pig had to be subjected to a brain scan prior to the start and at the of the season, yours truly included.

So I went in for my scan. Being a curious young man I asked the doctor what he was looking for and I discovered that the human body wasn't made to play football (duh). As it was explained to me the human brain sort of floats inside skull and it is surrounded by a fluid that allows for this "floating". In addition, this fluid acts as a conductor that allows electrical stimulation to take place. This, in turn, allows each human the ability to move, respond, and act at a reasonable pace.

Now, I'm sure that there are plenty of Michigan fans and graduates reading this so therefore there are plenty of doctors reading this chapter. I am not a doctor! All I'm telling you what was relayed to me, as I was about to become a "guinea pig". The doctor went on to say that a concussion was when the brain bounced off the side of the skull.

This is usually caused by a violent collision (something that the human body isn't supposed to do....... especially on a regular basis). He continued to say that even so the body has a wonderful way reacting to this type of injury. The liquid that the brain sits in starts to thicken around the bruised area, in essence it becomes like a soft cushion or padding so the brain can't "bounce" off that area again. The doctor then went on to say that football players tend to have the entire liquid area around the brain solidify because of all of the hitting. This process takes about two weeks for the brain to completely solidify. The ramifications meanwhile are serious. First, when the fluid solidifies the brain stays basically in one place, retarding the electrical pathways and sometimes impacting reaction time. In serious cases, if continued over long periods of time, there can be permanent damage.... With ex boxers when they had trouble responding, we called them "punch drunk".

About five days after my scan I was called back to the doctor's office. He told me there was good news and bad news. The good news was I was already "solidified". Meaning my brain liquid was already turned into a gel (that must have been from the hard hitting double sessions I just went through). I was thinking, "If this is the good news, damn, I didn't want to hear the bad news." The bad news he gave me really wasn't bad; in fact, it was good news to me. He said that because my brain fluid was now a gel I didn't have to do the full study. They really wanted guys who had not yet gelled. So I was off the hook for more than half the study. The most critical thing was that they wanted to test me after the season to see how quickly I returned to a fluid state.

In reality, when you're 18 years old a lot of this stuff is....well, stuff. You really don't care about it. I had made it through a full year with the team and I was starting to feel like one of the guys. I was starting to feel like I was invincible, so this mumbo jumbo about my brain really didn't bother me. There was no way anyone could tell me that I was slower to react than a year ago. I felt good.

I asked the doctor how long would it be before I returned to a normal liquefied state and he told me that would probably be about two or three months after I stopped hitting. That made me laugh, because with the fall season, spring ball, and next season double sessions I'd never have a three-month period without hitting. So I told myself, "Well, Curt, gel away!" I loved what I was doing and nobody; I mean nobody was going to convince me otherwise.

The great thing about this is now I have a permanent excuse if I ever forget anyone's name or do something really slow or stupid. I guess I have to thank Michigan for that too!

Even so, I've said this a thousand times. I wouldn't trade a second of those good times for a lifetime somewhere else.

CHAPTER 17

ACADEMICS

Not everything about playing football for Michigan is fun and games. You can only have so much fun smashing each other in practice, sweating, bleeding, running, lifting weights and getting hollered at three to four hours every day. When all that fun was over you still had to go to school.

I had some wonderful classes at Michigan. Some were very challenging. Some were very interesting. Some I attended knowing I would never use the information that I received once I left the University. All in all though, it was a great experience.

That said, the class that had the most impact on me was Anatomy. My goal was always to play football for Bo and for Michigan. If that didn't work out I was going to either be a doctor or a football coach (yes, it is true that 30 some years later neither came close to becoming reality). Bottom line though was that if you wanted to be a doctor you had to take Anatomy. So my sophomore year I signed up for the class.

The very first day I was assigned a green box that was about two and a half feet long and ten inches wide. Inside the box were most of the bones of some guy named "George". He had left his skeleton to the University so that future medical students could study ....bones. The box didn't contain a skull or pelvis and all of the bones had been sealed with lacquer to preserve them.

My first assignment was to learn every bone, where every muscle attached to each bone, where all the nerves and blood supply entered the bones and exited the bones. I started learning new words like "distal, proximal, medial, lateral", and all kinds of other good and important stuff. It was extremely interesting and held my attention almost as much as a good tongue lashing by Bo.

I used to keep George under my bed and pull the box out late at night and test myself on everything I was supposed to know. After a month we turned the box in and we were introduced to our lab. This was where my relationship with "Bessie" began. Bessie was my cadaver. She, too, had donated her remains to the University so that Michigan could train future surgeons and doctors. With that I have to stop and publicly apologize to Bessie. I did not become a doctor or surgeon. However, Bessie, you enhanced my appreciation for the human body and gave me one of the most profound experiences I've ever had.

When I met Bessie she was completely wrapped in plastic and a sheet. The attached card told me her first name only, that she was 63 when she died in 1974 and she had died due to pulmonary failure (her lungs couldn't transfer oxygen into her bloodstream) and eventually the lungs stopped and her heart stopped roughly the same time. My job was to use her to increase my education of the body and to return her (and the various parts) to her family when I was finished for burial. Hence, I had to save everything in a bucket at the end of the table.

After each session we washed and cleaned the areas we were working on to keep the body moist and returned it to the morgue slab. The class was approximately 30 students and we had ten cadavers. So there were three students to each cadaver. My two team members were both girls (nursing students) and they transferred out after two weeks so it was just Bessie and me.

Not all of the cadavers were there by wish. What I mean by that is that most had left their body to science but there were two or three that were " John or Jane Doe" that no one had claimed, so the surrounding cities' morgues gave the bodies to Michigan for research work. This fact is important to the rest of the story, but at this time I need to warn you that if you are at all squeamish please go ahead and skip this chapter.

The teaching doctor had us use each cadaver for studying specific parts of the body. As an example, we would use one cadaver when we were studying all of the musculature of the leg. The doctor would dissect this area and we would observe, then we would go back to our own cadaver and commence the same dissection procedure.

By the end of the first semester we had covered the thorax or chest area and all of those internal organs. We also did the digestive system and all the organs, blood supply and nerves for that area. We had also done all of the muscles, veins, and nerves of the back, legs and arms.

There really were only a couple of things that stand out in my mind as being "uncomfortable". The first was the removal of fat tissue. Fat in the human body looks similar to tapioca pudding and it was months before I could eat that again. The second was some of the odors that come from out of all of this stuff. It isn't pleasant and you really have to get used to it.

With that, my defining moment was when the doctor advised us that we were going to get into the "cranium". He wanted to do this in two different fashions. The first was to provide for a "transverse" section of the head. The cadaver next to Bessie and me was a young man who was about my age (18 at the time) when he met his demise. He had been shot with a shotgun and was missing a quarter of the right side of his head. He was one of those "John Does" that no one ever claimed. However, in his state, we couldn't use John for the cranium exercise.

The doctor asked me if I was willing to allow the class use Bessie for this particular session. Mind you, that after all the dissection procedures the only things that remained attached to her head were the spinal vertebrae, the right clavicle, scapula and humerus with minor tendons, pelvis and skin from where the legs used to be. Unfortunately the doctor had to leave the lab for a few minutes but he asked me to cut transversely through the head and skull so that we could see a right and left side (so basically in half).

I dare say that there aren't too many people that have ever had to do this but the doctor was matter of fact in his request. I asked what I was to use to accomplish the task and I was handed a hacksaw. Now, Bessie in her prime weighed in at about 110 pounds. Now, unfortunately she was about 25-30 pounds. Since there were no muscles or weight to allow me to anchor I had to put her head on a block of wood and I had to climb up on the cold metal slab and pin her remaining bones down with my knees.

When I started the back and forth sawing motion it made a few of the other students sick. In addition, I was in such a hurry to get this over with I sawed as fast as I could. In doing so the bone began to smoke and there was the most God-awful smell that filled the room. It must have been an amazing sight for the rest of the class.

When the doctor came back in he complemented me on the speed in which I accomplished the task. I asked him if I could excuse myself and I went over to the sink and ran cold water over my head for a few minutes. Though it sounds revolting looking at one half of a human head with all of the amazing things- brain area, nerves, bone, and sinus cavities- was amazing. Getting to look inside the human body made me realize how simply we are put together. Even more remarkable is that all of this stuff functions so smoothly.

I have been blessed in my life. I had a fine athletic career, and a wonderful business career. I am happily married to the same wonderful woman for going on three decades. I have healthy and prospering children. What I have been through has been a great blessing and an experience I'll never forget or replace. As simple as I am and similar in stature to everyone else, it helps make me feel unique and fortunate.

CHAPTER 18
GOOD EATS

Michigan football in 1974 is nowhere near what it is today. Now don't get me wrong -- a scholarship in 1974 was great, too. The way it worked back then was if you lived in a dorm, your room, board, books, and classes were covered by the scholarship. During the season, dinners were provided at training table and on Saturday and Sunday you were given vouchers to eat at Steak and Four Restaurant out near the highway.

If you lived in an apartment, classes, books and training table were taken care of and you were given a monthly check that you had to budget for your extra food and apartment. I can't remember the exact amount but the monthly check was around $300. So, if you found a 2-bedroom apartment (split 4 ways) for $600 per month and threw in another $50 for utilities and phone it basically left you with $40 a week for entertainment and food.

Hence, we became experts on *all* the deals in and around Ann Arbor. We could have told you where every "all you can eat" joint was and we had the places that would "spiff" extras. There was this one place called "Steve's Lunch" on University next to what was the Village Bell. Steve made great omelets. Steve was awesome. He was this tiny Asian guy that loved Michigan football.

Steve's "spiff" was to max out our omelets. So, we would order a regular 3 egg omelet and it would come back with ham, bacon, cheese, peppers, mushrooms, hash browns and toast (and it was probably closer to a 5 egg deal). We paid for what was considered a "regular". It was sweet. Every Sunday morning he had a line outside the shop because everyone knew some ball players were going to show.

To stretch our dollars, my roommates and I decided the best thing for us to do was to pool our money and go to Meijer's Thrifty Acres to buy as much as we could in bulk. I realized shortly after the first trip I realized that I got the short end of the stick. One morning I came down and Mike Kenn ("Big Fella") was having his own breakfast. It consisted of a dozen eggs, half a loaf of bread, a quart of orange juice, a quart of milk and a half pound of bacon. I knew then I was in for a losing battle by pooling our dough. So it was back to trying to find the all you can eat joints.

There was one out on Huron Road that had all you could eat on Sundays for $3.95. The owner set out a steel bin of chicken breasts, a bin of pork chops, and a bin of spaghetti. When Big Fella took the entire bin we thought we might get in trouble. He looked pretty funny with a steel bin in front of him instead of a plate.

After an hour the owner came over and told us he'd refund our money if we'd just leave. Mike ate about 30 chicken breasts! We got our money's worth that night. Those were good times indeed.

CHAPTER 19

ALMOST IN

Put this one in the strange but true category. I was red shirted in 1974, part of the deal I made with Bo early in the early part of the season. Red shirting stinks because you practice with the team just as if you were preparing for a game but deep in your heart you know you'll never get to play, not even if it was a blowout (and we had plenty of them)!

Sometimes I wonder how many career yards Rob Lytle would have ended up with had he played all four quarters of every game. He sat through half of all the games in 1975 and 1976 watching others play because we were so far ahead and didn't need him. You'll see his name up there in total rushing yards but not carries.

Anyway, I spent my red shirt year as pounding meat on the scout team for All American's Dave Brown and Don Dufek. Every other week I was brought up to run with the first two teams on offense but the starting receivers were Gil Chapman (wingback) and Jim Smith (split end). The second team was Keith Johnson (split end) and Jim Smith (wingback). We went 10-0 that year heading in to the show down at the horseshoe against Ohio State.

We had a great week of practice, even though I spent the whole week on the scout team. I felt in my heart our defense was primed to keep the Buckeyes out of our end zone. After practice on Thursday we heard that Chapman's hamstring was really sore but no big deal. Friday, the travel squad left early on a flight to Columbus. The rest of us made plans for the weekend. Mine included jumping in a car with John Ceddia ("Seed") our scout team quarterback to drive to Columbus to see the game.

We arrived around 7:00 p.m., just in time for Seed to take me to a frat party. He was from Ohio, so he had a few friends at OSU. Boy, what a mistake! I never saw so many drunks. The parties spilled over on to High Street. They were turning over cars and starting fires.

I made it back to the hotel not soon enough. In the lobby I ran into Tirrell Burton, my position coach. He told me that Jim Smith, while diving for a pass at practice today, had separated his shoulder and they had been looking for me all over Ann Arbor to tell me to drive down. There were no cell phones then. Jon Falk had already made arrangements for my pads and they were in route. They were being driven down by an equipment manager that night.

I met with Bo around 10:30 pm and he simply asked if I was ready to go. He said I wouldn't suit up but "just be ready." So for the first 25 minutes of the game I stood behind the bench in street clothes and watched a classic battle. OSU couldn't get inside our 20yard line if the world depended on it. With 5 minutes to go in the first half Keith Johnson got knocked out with a concussion. Bo hollered to Falk to get me ready.

We were escorted by Ohio's finest back to the locker room. By the time the team came in I was taped and half suited. I knew this was my moment. Even though I was going to blow an entire year of eligibility I was willing to do so to beat Ohio State. I was as high on adrenalin as humanly possible, ready to make my mark.

Bo, though, had other ideas. He came over as I finished dressing and said, "No, we're going with double tights" (meaning two tight ends and Chapman would be the only wide out). I slowly got undressed and went from one of the highest highs to the lowest lows as OSU kicked 4 field goals and beat us 12-10. Even though we lost, we still tied for the title as OSU had previously lost to MSU.

My potential moment had come and gone, but there were other opportunities still to come and I was prepared to make the most of them. Even though the emotional swings were devastating I wouldn't trade it for any amount of money. This was a good time, rare but good.

CHAPTER 20

You're Fired

Preparing for the 1975 season was a challenge. We had gone 10-0-1 in '73 and 10-1 in '74 and hadn't gone to a bowl game. We entered the spring with only one returning starting defensive back, Don Dufek and it looked like we were going to start two to three sophomores (Dwight Hicks, Jim Pickens or Derek Howard).

We were loaded with running backs, however, including Gordon Bell and Rob Lytle, and two heralded ones coming in, Harlan Huckleby and Russell Davis. While there was a host of others including Mike Smith, Dennis Richardson, and Max Richardson on the roster. That prompted Bo and Jack Harbaugh to spend the better part of spring ball looking to shore up the secondary.

One guy who transformed himself into a good wide corner was former tailback, Jimmy Bolden, but it wasn't enough. During one very slow and painful scrimmage Bo finally lost it and started yelling that he needed someone, anyone, to play in the secondary and Harbaugh came over to scout out the receivers.

Jim Smith was our stud so he wasn't going anywhere. Rick White (6'5", 220 pounds) was too big and bulky. So Harbaugh focused on Keith Johnson and me. He hounded us the rest of practice. When we got to the locker room (ah, to be warm again, that was always a treat), he followed us right to our locker. He grabbed me and asked if I had ever played on the defensive side of the ball. I told him that I had played safety in high

52

school, but someone was looking down upon me and Bo (bless him) interceded and told Coach Harbaugh that I was off limits.

Harbaugh immediately asked Keith if he knew the calls on defense. Keith was a great guy from a small town in Indiana and he had a really dry sense of humor. He asked Coach Harbaugh to test him on the calls. So Harbaugh asked Keith," What to you do on a 70 Jump?" Keith immediately squatted down and jumped up in the air as high as he could. In the process he hit his head on the door jam and the entire room fell down laughing. All we heard from Harbaugh was, "Shit, Johnson, you're fired!"

He and Bo would simply have to start sophomores the next year.

CHAPTER 21
BLUE WHITE GAME

By the end of Spring Football in April 1975 there were some valid reasons for me to be excited about my future with Michigan football. We were about to play the annual Blue White football game. This was where the coaches divided up the teams basically through draft choices and half of the team wore blue jerseys and half wore white jerseys and we played a full blown game in the stadium.

The reason I was excited was that I had both a scholarship and had burned my redshirt so the only way that I wasn't going to get on the field now was because I wasn't good enough to play. Over the past year I had worked my way up to the third team split end and because I knew both the flanker and split end positions I was really more like second team. Gil Chapman was graduating so the only guys left were Jim Smith, Keith Johnson, Rick White and me. There were others but they didn't play both positions.

Truth be told, Smitty was almost exclusively a wingback. Other guys who had a shot were Andy Jackson, Max Richardson and Jerry Collins. Collins and Jackson only played split end and Max only played wing so I had a chance to see some real action if I could prove myself.

The coaches split the team up. Gary Moeller was the head coach of the white team and Jerry Hanlon was the head coach of the blue team. Bo was supposed to be a bystander but he ended up calling the plays for both sides and if he wanted to trade a player for another or see a player with a different group, the trade went through by merely switching jerseys. The other neat thing about this game was that the winners got to eat steak after and the losers got hot dogs. It made it extra funny when the dinner was being dished out because everyone would always claim that at some point in the game Bo had traded them to the winning team. It was always a hoot to hear the bellyaching going on if you didn't get a steak!

I don't remember the score and I know I didn't catch any passes but I had a pretty good day blocking and knew that I would be judged well after the game. The most amazing thing though was that after years of having Dennis Franklin as our quarterback there was only one guy who had a shot at the top job and that was Mark Elzinga, or "Z" to everyone. The 1975 season was going to be unique as we only had a few proven returning stars.

Everyone knew that we would have a new center, new guards, and maybe new tight ends. Rob Lytle would be the fullback and Gordie Bell the tailback. Jim Smith would be one receiver and Keith Johnson the other. The word was out. Maybe, just maybe we would try a new guy at quarterback. Maybe it would be a new kid coming in as a freshman.

It had never been done before, start a freshman a quarterback at Michigan. I didn't think it would happen, Z was a good quarterback and he ran the option pretty well. But we knew the1975 team would truly be unique as we would have some new players at many positions. I was both apprehensive and jacked up at the same time. Regardless of whatever was going to be new, my goal, my heart told me that I would be part of this new look.

CHAPTER 22

CROSS COUNTRY AGAIN

The decision to go home in the summer of 1975 was one I struggled with because there was so much to risk. I decided to drive back to California in late April 1975. My body craved the beach and the ocean plus there were two girls from my high school who had really caught my attention by writing me letters, wooing me back to La Jolla.

My mind screamed at me, "Don't go, don't go. Stay in Ann Arbor, get a job, work out with the team and earn your spot!" In the end I thought that I had a good work out schedule that I was following and I was certain that I would return in shape and win the "Best Conditioned Athlete" so I drove across country, again.

Most of the things that needed to be taken care of were already handled. I had recorded excellent grades. My apartment for the following season was already arranged and I was going to be living with football players. We had taken a lease for the fall on South Forrest, unit 23. My roommates were going to be Eric Phelps, a defensive end, Rex Mackel , a linebacker, and Mike Kenn, a tackle.

We were all scholarship players. Eric and I had previously met, both on the field and we were in Anatomy class together. We were from different coasts but had hit it off and soon were hanging together.

I figured that I'd be OK going back home ....wait a minute! My parents had moved from La Jolla up the coast to Del Mar just as I was reporting to football camp last July. This was going to be a new deal. I would be driving to a new home, new room, and new area. The trip was uneventful and I made it with ease in three days.

I started out on my same routine of running, volleyball and having Bookie throw me a ton of passes, but this summer I added a weigh lifting routine. I signed up to lift weights at Maylen's Gym in La Jolla. Maylen was the guy who used to be the strength coach for the San Diego Chargers and he ran informal practices for high school kids in the summer. It was good that I was hanging with guys who were in to football.

I knew I needed to add the lifting routine because Michigan had dropped the Universal gym and had installed a new weight room full of Nautilus equipment. This was under direction of Coach Tom Reed , who was the new defensive line coach and a work out type of guy. It was obvious that we were moving to a system where we would have a full time strength and conditioning coach.

Yep, a lot of things were going to be different but through the summer I logged hundreds of miles on the coast and through the soft sand beaches. When I got in my car to return to Ann Arbor in late summer 1975 I was ready to fight for playing time.

CHAPTER 23
BEST CONDITIONED

When we all arrived on campus in August 1975, there was change in the air. First, we were told that the preseason testing would be different than it was before. We were going to be tested in repeat 40- yard dashes, 1.5 mile run, bench press, military press, dips, pull ups and two kinds of shuttle cone races. This was far more serious than how we had been tested the year before.

All of these tests would be administered over two days in between meetings. The first day we'd run the 1.5 miles in the morning and do the lifts before the afternoon practice. The second day we'd do the 40s in the morning and the cones just prior to the afternoon practice. Another change, which was a ritual, was watching all the new freshmen come in to the dorms. This class had some real solid looking players. There was Russell Davis who looked like he could play in the NFL right away, as did Mel Owens a fully built linebacker out of Chicago.

Then there were the three Detroit Cass Tech guys. Each of them, Harlan Huckleby, Curt Greer and Tom Seabron looked like race horses. There were also two big tight ends in Mark Smerge and Gene Johnson, though most of us wanted to see Johnson's high school teammate from Flint, Rick Leach.

He certainly wasn't any bigger than Dennis Franklin. He looked about my size. His times in the 40 and 1.5 mile wouldn't have impressed anyone yet there was a way that he picked up running the option that showed this kid knew what he was doing, even if it was without pads.

As we went through the various events I asked some of the graduate assistant coaches how they were going to score things. There was to be points for lifting 225 pounds 1-5 times, 6-10 times, 11-15 times and so on. The same was true for dips, and pull ups. You also got points for certain times in the cones and you received points for the number of times you ran your forties within a half second of you fastest time. The 1.5 mile was unique. We were told that you'd get points for running it under 10 minutes and you'd get more points for every 10 seconds under that time. After we ran the first day Barry Pierson, a graduate assistant coach, told me I had already amassed more points on my 1.5 mile time than the rest of all the tests had available combined.

That meant two things. The first was that I was going to be crowned, "Best Conditioned Athlete." The second was that they would have to restructure the scoring system in the future. By the time we finished the tests I was fairly confident I would never be on the scout team again. Now I had to prove myself to the coaches that I belonged in the game.

I actually looked forward to these practices and double sessions in 1975 because my confidence was high. I was putting up times that no one in the history of Michigan football had ever posted before, at least not for football players. When you have confidence that you can compete with what is thought to be the, "best of the best" it allows you to break through any barriers that might have normally held you back.

I had a few things going for me now. I had a nickname, "Surf", I had a title, "Best Conditioned Athlete," I had a full ride, and I had the coaches attention. There was a general feeling that there was no stopping me now. That felt great!

CHAPTER 24
BEHIND THE SCENES

There was plenty of stuff that went on behind the scenes that no one ever hears about – or, frankly, cares about - that revolves around Michigan football. The medical side is one of these things.

Every football player at Michigan is poked and prodded beyond belief to make sure that they are in physical condition to be subject to the game itself. Every year that I played for Michigan I went through numerous physical inspections that became routine. One of the rare moments came just before the 1975 season began. By this time I was on full scholarship and every player, both walk-ons and full rides, had to have total physicals before the season began. This included examination of every moving part of your body and some parts, even, that don't move.

I remember being the first in line for the blood tests. There was probably 30 guys waiting behind me and I was followed directly by Jim Bolden. As I stepped up to have blood drawn I was told by the head nurse that I would be giving three vials of blood. Since there were so many players to give blood this would be a good opportunity for the nursing school to train upcoming nurses in the art of taking blood. So, again, I became a guinea pig.

We were all standing in our half shirts and shorts, making jokes about what was ahead of us.... primarily the "look away and cough" routine. I sat down at one of the school desks that had the flip up writing board. The head nurse looked on as she instructed a rookie nurse to advise me to make a fist. I remember her saying to the rookie nurse, "don't worry -- you won't hurt him. He's a big strong man".

The rookie nurse plunged the needle into my arm and she went right through the vein in my left arm. The head nurse told her that was ok and to just fish around until she penetrated the vein. Finally she was able to do that and the vial filled quickly.

The next maneuver was a tricky one. The rookie nurse had to pull the vial out and attach a new vial while leaving the needle in my arm. I guess she got a little nervous and she pulled the vial out without the rubber stopper that capped the vial. The result? The entire vial spilled over the desktop. With blood dripping down the desk and on to the floor she tried to insert a new vial and pushed the needle right through to the middle of my elbow. Bolden then turned to the rest of the thirty guys in line and blurted out, "She's trying to murder us".

That was the last thing the rookie nurse needed to hear, and she began to cry. Jimmy turned to the head nurse and said, "She's not getting near *me* with a needle," and the whole place burst out laughing. This didn't help matters at all.

Throughout the entire ordeal, all had forgotten about me, and as I looked down I saw that I still had a needle in my arm but no vial. With every heart beat I could see a new spurt of blood jet out on to the desk top. Finally, the head nurse took over and finished the job. She then gave me a swab to cover the hole in my arm and they stopped the procedure to clean up all the blood on the desk and the floor.

When I arose to go to the next station for another part of the physical there were no Michigan football players left in the room. They had all split, wanting no part of what they had just witnessed.

CHAPTER 25
HEAD KNOCKING

It was early in the season 1975. We were playing with a freshman quarterback and starting two sophomores on the offensive line. I had been redshirted in 1974 and was looking for my first serious playing time.

We really struggled in the first few games coming away with one win and two ties. After finishing the previous two years with only one loss starting out 1975 at 1-0-2 left a lot of folks screaming for Bo's and Leach's heads on platters. It was very hard to listen or read the papers as everyone was a "doubting Thomas".

We made some subtle changes. Mark Elzinga took a few series at quarterback and we inserted "Big Fella" Mike Kenn at tackle, a position he wouldn't relinquish until he graduated in 1978. Bo even put me in on most of the special teams. I played end on the punt teams and was also thrown in on the kick return team against Missouri. I'd never done that before as I'd always returned the kick offs in high school. But now I was part of "the wedge".

So when we opened the second half we trotted out on to the field and the kick came down I formed up on the end of the wedge and we all waited for the call. When the returner caught the ball and was 10-15 yards behind us he'd yell "go" and we would make a mad dash up the field trying to run over anyone that came our way. I heard the "go" and I started to run as fast as I could, looking for someone to hit. Looking up I saw Missouri's "wedge buster". This is the guy that acts as if he's a kamikaze and attempts to destroy the wedge so other players can come in and make the tackle.

This particular wedge buster must have been 6'3" 230 pounds and since I was 6'1", 185 pounds he picked me out as the one he'd throw his body up against. You couldn't blame him. I would have done the same thing if the roles were reversed. A few things go through your mind at this juncture and this is one of those moments in time where you have to take stock of yourself. There is not a lot of time but you do have the chance to tell yourself, "well this is it let's see what you are made of".

I felt a need to prove myself to Bo and the rest of the team so I charged ahead willing to meet the Missouri player head on. About 10 yards from impact I lowered my head at the same time he lowered his. Our helmets hit flush at full speed and I flew back about three yards. When I got up and tried to gather my senses everything seemed to be in slow motion. I knew I had to make it back to the huddle for the next play so I staggered to the huddle and put my hands on my knees to steady myself.

The ground seemed to be rolling. I was hoping no one in the huddle would notice that I was out on my feet. I looked to my right and half of the huddle was laughing. They all knew I was loopy as cat on catnip. I looked to my left and had to stare real hard. I was looking right at the Missouri linebacker. He was in our huddle and didn't have a clue where he was either. As a matter of fact he looked way worse than me!

Leach sent me to the bench and I was back in the groove within 10 minutes but the other guy had to be helped off the field. I figured I had passed my first "on the field test". That's what football is all about, knocking a few heads in!

CHAPTER 26

FEAR

Sometimes fear is a good thing. A lot of guys feared Bo, but his kind of fear made you do things that you wouldn't ordinarily accomplish. I have to admit I still have dreams where he commands the legions and if he were in front of me today asking me to do something for him, I'd be asking him, how much, how high, how far!

Still even more feared Michigan. In 1975 we resumed a series with Northwestern and candidly, they were a doormat of the Big Ten. They had a pretty good safety back then named Pete Shaw. He went on to something like an eight year career with the San Diego Chargers. At a recent NFL Retired Players Golf Tournament he pulled me aside and reminded me of that fear. He told me that their whole team dreaded coming to the Big House. They dreaded the machine they were about to face.

He told me that Bo had recruited him and during the recruitment had challenged him if he was good enough to play at "Michigan". Pete said he never believed there was that much difference until the day he came to Ann Arbor to take on the Wolverines.

I remember the game. My job was to "cut" any DB that came up to try and stop our option. Today, cutting out a player's knees is illegal but back then we used to get a "K" on our scorecard if we succeeded (every player is graded on overall performance on every play). A "K" on a receiver's card meant you had a "knockdown". That was cutting the defensive player's knees out and knocking him down.

By the start of the third quarter I had 11 "K's" and most of them were on Pete. On my 12th K Pete got up and said he had enough. He said he would run off the field or go anywhere I wanted him to go and he promised he wouldn't even try to tackle anyone if we would just leave his knees alone. After this series I was pulled from the game and other receivers finished out, but not before I told everyone about the deal Pete and I cut. During the films the next day we were all laughing so hard because of how silly the Northwestern backs looked following every receiver all over the field, anywhere except near the ball! That was a different kind of fear. Different from what even Bo wanted.

CHAPTER 27

My First Autograph

One of the neat things that happen when you play for a big time program like Michigan is the recognition. I'll admit I never really thought about it much as a youngster while I was dreaming of playing for the Wolverines but I can tell you exactly where I was when I was asked to sign my first autograph.

I also know where I was when I got my first fan letter. The summer of 1975, our first full pad practice of double sessions, I was standing in front of my locker and I got my first piece of fan mail. There was a space right above where you hung your clothes for valuables. It was right under your nameplate. When I looked up it was staring right back at me.

Back then, of course, we didn't have text messaging, emails or cell phones, so if someone wanted to get a hold of you and didn't know where to write they just wrote to " so and so" care of Michigan Football, Ann Arbor. You'd be amazed how many letters got through to players with only their name and Michigan football.

The letter was right next to my roll, which was a tightly wrapped combination of a Michigan football half shirt, shorts, jock and socks that equipment manager Jon Falk had washed and prepared the night before, so I sat down on my stool and opened the letter. I had a big smile on my face as this was a pretty big step for an unknown former walk-on. The letter was crudely worded, mostly misspelled but I was going to cherish

66

it. It basically said that the letter writer had been following me, thought I was a good player and wanted me to write him back.

Later that evening in the dorm I penned a response and mailed it the next day. I figured the author had to be seven or eight years old. About a week later I received another letter from the kid and I responded in return. After a month of letters every week I received a letter from the same address (it was from Gaylord, Michigan). The letter was from the boy's father telling me how wonderful it was that I responded since I was the only one who did. His son had been writing letters to athletes from Michigan State, the Detroit Tigers, Detroit Lions, etc. The father went on to say his son was a huge sports fan but there was a slight problem. His son was 45 years old and had a severe learning disability and would never mentally get beyond the capacity of an eight or nine year old.

Back in 1975, the Athletic Department's policy was to provide complimentary tickets to the players. If you were a freshman you got two tickets to each game, sophomores got two, juniors got three and seniors received four. Hell, I was from California and hardly ever needed my tickets, so I always gave them away to my roommates. They always needed them as their families routinely came to the games.

But this particular family had touched me, so I wrote back and told the dad that I would put two tickets to the next Michigan game in their name at will call. After the game, I met them outside our locker room. We had just beaten Northwestern 69-0 and the father and son were on cloud nine.

I remember the great big smile on his face as we shook hands. I was 19 and he was 45 (five years older than my dad at the time). He had one simple request, "Mr. Stephenson," he asked humbly, "Can I have your autograph?" I won't ever forget that moment, forever.

CHAPTER 28
CRAZY REX

In 1975 I resided at an apartment complex on South Forrest. Our unit number was No.23, so we referred to ourselves as members of "Club 23". That was to differentiate us from the Arch Street Athletic Club, which was where the Dufeks (Donny and Billy) and six other players lived down the street. In addition, three apartments down, Club17 housed the Chicago boys Gerry Szara, Mark ("Paw") Donohue, Bobby ("Langer") Lang, and Jim ("Hack") Hackett. Jim Hackett was actually from Ohio but acted like the "boyz from Chytown".

So we were all a few blocks from each other and could rumble over to the practice field in less than five minutes. Bo had a schedule to maintain, after all and you wouldn't dare be late for anything! My roommates were Mike Kenn (Big Fella"), Eric Phelps and Rex Mackal ("Crazy"). We each had our quirks but got along great.

You all know that I was "Surf" because I was from California. Rex was unique in many ways. Some of his secrets will have to remain forever untold, but others we can divulge. He had this big red afro when he reported as a freshman in 1974 (remember it was the '70s). His hair must have been 16 inches long but was really curly so he combed it into a huge afro.

I remember he walked into the meeting room on the first day and went right up to Chuck Heater. Seniors sat in the first row and Heater sat in the first seat in the first row so everyone in the room saw what happened. Rex, who was a linebacker, stuck his finger in Heater's chest and announced, " Look out brother cause here I come". Half the team thought he was nuts and the other half thought Heater was going to kill him. Quite a first impression!

That night, Rex went downtown and might have had a few too many. He passed out on to one of those candles that are put on the tables and his hair caught on fire. Les Miles, one of our offensive linemen at the time put it out with a pitcher of beer. The next day, Rex came into the meeting room with his head shaved. After that he was simply know as "Crazy".

One of the crazy things he would do was to speak in lyrics of songs, instead of good old English. You had to be an aficionado of the music of the time to understand him. After his head caught on fire he was asked how he felt and his reply was, "Don't ask what kind of shape I'm in, ain't pretty, can't sing and my legs are thin. Don't ask me what I think of you I won't give the answers that you want me to" (Fleetwood Mac).

During double sessions his last year he was really dragging and was asked by a coach if he still liked football (sarcastically of course). Crazy replied, "We are programmed to receive, you can check out anytime you like but you can never leave" (Eagles). The coach just rolled his eyes! One of my favorites was when he was in a cast because he had fractured his elbow and was asked if we could get him something to eat. Rex responded (in song of course), "My favorite flavor cheery aid, I sung my song to Mr. Jimmy and this is what he said you can't always get what you want, you can't always get what you want but if you try some time, you'll find you get what you need." (Rolling Stones)

We ordered him some pizza from a new place that had just opened in Ann Arbor. It was called Dominos.

On a bet, he walked/climbed the window sills half way around West Quad about 40 feet off the ground, so just about everything he did was crazy. Once, in the middle of winter, Rex gave me a ride. I was supposed to meet my girlfriend some place and when I got into Rex's car I knew I wasn't going to make it there on time. The roads were icy and slick. He had his music blaring from the radio full blast and he was singing along. As he picked up speed he purposely looked for ice patches so he could slam on the brakes and cause the car to skid. Luckily he was a skilled driver! A little way outside Ann Arbor (which was NOT the direction

I wanted to go) he told me we were going to do something really cool. In a few minutes I found myself looking down a hill towards a small lake that looked frozen. Sure enough Rex hollered, "Gimme a ticket for an airplane" in unison with Joe Cocker on the radio and floored his car toward the lake. When we hit the surface he hit the brakes and we must have done six to eight 360 - degree circles, just like a spinning top! All the way across the lake! To this day I'm glad the lake was frozen solid. When we stopped he was laughing his head off and I was looking for mine!

It takes all kinds to play this crazy game we all love so much and Rex was a kind of his own. Although it really was a lot of fun, he provided some moments I know I'll never experience again…and I know I don't want to.

CHAPTER 29
GOING BOWLING

There were smiles all around. We had just finished singing The Victors in the visiting locker room in Champaign Urbana after beating Illinois 21-15. We were undefeated with a few warts as we were 8-0-2.

The best news though was that the winner of next week's game against Ohio State was going to go to the Rose Bowl. Bo held our attention longer than usual after a game. He looked around the room and got that "I am as serious as hell look on his face" and said, "Gentlemen, what you accomplished today and this season cannot go unrewarded. I faced 90 Wolverines two years ago and had to tell them they were staying home for the holidays even though they were the best-damned football team in America. Last year, I had to face another 90 Wolverines and tell them that their conference wouldn't allow them to play over the holidays even though they had gone 20-1-1 in two years of football."

Bo told us he was never going to let that happen again, especially this year. Then he told us why.

"I am here to tell you that no matter what happens next week you are going to be playing football on New Year's Day. I don't like it but we had to change the system. I made a deal yesterday that if we beat Ohio State next week Michigan will play in the Rose Bowl, but if we don't we will accept a bid to play in the Orange Bowl. You deserve to know this and it has already been arranged. One week to go now, so let's really get after it next week."

71

Part of me was stunned and not in a good way. I was still too young to understand schedules, logistics and negotiations. That was for someone else to figure out. What was stunning for me was that Bo would have even gone into some negotiation that included us not winning. That was a startling revelation for me. Then came the realization that I would never, ever feel like I did the previous two seasons.

Bo had accomplished a miracle. Michigan would play in a bowl game......from now until forever. The concept of not having a winning season isn't even fathomable even to this day. It seemed as if it was all worth it now. The long runs, the sweat, the pain, the blood........God, I was going to be in a bowl game!

Sure, I wanted the Rose Bowl, but now everyone in La Jolla would know I made it. Remember that the only TV games that were seen in California were the Ohio State game and the bowl game. This was great. I couldn't wait to get home and call my parents and tell them.

CHAPTER 30

OSU 1975

We entered the game undefeated but with two blemishes, a pair of ties with Baylor and Stanford. We should have won both games but then again we had started a freshman quarterback for the first time in Michigan history. Having a freshman run a complicated option offense was nearly a miracle in itself, but to go undefeated was an astonishing feat.

Bo had told us the week before that he had cut a deal, win or lose we were going to a bowl game. Even with a freshman quarterback, a sophomore line, and our defense was going up against the greatest player in the history of OSU football we expected to win. For 54 minutes it was a hell of a game. Donny Dufek owned Archie Griffin that day. I mean he absolutely *owned* him. Archie had run for over 100 yards in every game he started except the 1974 Michigan game. Well, in 1975 he didn't even gain 40 yards. Dufek physically beat him up.

If you watch video of the 1976 Rose Bowl you'll see Archie leaving the game physically unable to perform. That wasn't because of UCLA hitting him. It was because he was nursing busted ribs from playing against Michigan and Dufek. We were ahead 14-7 and had OSU pinned down near their own end zone. It was something like 3rd and 15 to go when Cornelius Green went back to pass. I watched Timmy Davis our middle guard slip his block and beat down on the OSU quarterback. I thought for sure TD was going to tackle Green for a safety and we would be headed to the Rose Bowl. Somehow Green escaped and rambled up the sideline for a first down.

A few plays later OSU scored to tie the game. After this the game was a blur. We got the ball back on our own 20 yard line with just a few minutes left. No one can blame Bo or Leach for what happened next. We had to gain yardage in big chunks because we couldn't play for a tie. A tie would give the Rose Bowl to Ohio, so we had to throw the ball. Well, disaster struck and OSU intercepted and ran it all the way back to our two yard line and punched in a TD after that. We went to a three receiver offense but we couldn't get a first down and lost 21-14.

Yes, this stung but not as much as the previous two years. We lost this game on the field, at least, not by a vote. I took some solace away that I'd be playing in the Orange Bowl and the fact that our running back, Gordie Bell, had a much better game than Archie, but not much. Sure, I was jacked that I'd be playing in a Bowl game. That would be great. But, it wasn't the Rose Bowl and we weren't champions. That would have to be in the future.

Bo Schembechler, Rick Leach, Curt Stephenson and Jim Smith celebrate a Michigan touchdown.

CHAPTER 31
FOOTBALL PLAYERS

My grandfather used to tell me, "Don't believe everything you hear". For years I have been hearing that football players at major colleges are supposed to be viewed in the same light as all other student athletes. We all know this is not true. They are treated differently, of course, sometimes this is good, sometimes this is bad.

Yes, I used to get preferential treatment when it came to class selection. Mostly this was to accommodate the schedule needed to allow me to participate in afternoon practices. Yes, my meals were paid for (once I was on scholarship anyway), my tuition, my room and board …but this was a lot less than what was being brought into the University every Saturday in the fall.

Yes, I had professors that, once they knew I was a football player gave me breaks to help me deal with my schedule, but I also had some that purposely made life harder. Some made crazy demands on meeting deadlines, some even graded harder. To me it all about evened out.

Through it all I can tell you one thing. Football players are not normal. There is different wiring inside their heads. Why else would they do what they do? I would be the last to tell you that they are superior to others. I've been around too many to make that statement and have read too many reports of the knucklehead maneuvers many have attempted or accomplished.

That said, being surrounded by them, being one of them, I have never laughed louder or harder. I have never tested my beliefs, my strength, my courage, my fears as completely and thoroughly with anyone else but football players. I have never been as high or as low with anyone else but football players. Some of the smartest men I have ever met have been football players and some of the dumbest have also played the game.

All that said, they are wired differently than the rest of the world. Why would a human being clasped arms with another human being and smack heads together until one was knocked unconscious (or quit)? The ritual of head butting has been a football mainstay for generations. It really gets unique when it's done without helmets. Why would anyone fill jock straps with heat balm, fill shoes with crap, or put hair remover in shampoo?

Take this quandary? You're a Michigan football player and you're going to the Orange Bowl. It's near the end of the term and you're not sure if you're going to get a passing grade in a certain class. The professor holds you after class and says, "I was thinking about going down to Florida over the break and I can "C" you down there at the game", as he writes a "C" on the blackboard. Do you put his name down for tickets at "will call"? Common sense says you don't for a number of reasons.

One, you didn't earn the grade. Two, that's cheating, still, you want to be eligible and play and if you don't pass this class that might not happen. Well, there is no telling how many players would respond to the situation with different answers. I can tell you that one accepted the offer, and was still given an "F", even after giving up the tickets. As this was going down I could hear the echoes in my head from my grandfather," don't believe everything you hear".

In the end justice, prevailed. The knucklehead player told Bo about the deal and after being in the dog house for four months, running steps for who knows how long, and making the class up in summer school he learned his lesson. As for the professor, he's long gone, asked to leave by the administration immediately. I presume it was because he would have never been able to get out of his own doghouse. Even if he could, do you think that professor would ever like to cross Bo's path?

CHAPTER 32

1975 ORANGE BOWL

Oklahoma took the field led by that crazy wagon pulled by horses. I could see Barry Switzer and the famous Selmon brothers, Dewey and Lee Roy on the other side of the field.

The first few series were slugfests with neither team getting any edge. On our second series we, again, bogged down and had to punt. Back in those days it was uncommon for the punting team to split out "gunners", which are routinely doubled teamed today. Everyone lined up in a tight formation and did the best that you could to protect the punter.

When we were watching film on Oklahoma, we noticed they would pinch down on the end of the line. This was because the fastest guy usually was out there to cover the punt. What Oklahoma did was leave the tackle uncovered (as we all know, tackles are suppose to be big and slow) and they would double up on the end. So on the second series when it came time to punt I switched positions with the tackle on our punt team. Sure enough I was uncovered and as soon as the ball was snapped I was off.

After about 20 yards I located the flight of the ball and there was no one near me. The receiver was Oklahoma's running back, Joe Washington. It looked as if I was going to get to him at exactly the same moment as the ball. Boy, this was going to look good on film as I prepared to take Joe's head off. Sure enough the ball, arrived a split second before I did. I lowered my head and committed the cardinal sin. I closed my eyes! I went airborne figuring it would highlight the hit. Joe somehow caught the ball and did a little shimmy where he turned sideways and all I got was half of my arm on his hip.

I flew through the air and landed face first of the astroturf. I don't think Joe got more than a few yards and was swarmed under by other Wolverines but did I look foolish on the film. I also took grief from all of my buddies back home after the game. "Nice air time" and "Hey, I always wanted to know what's it feels like to lose you jock?"

Fortunately for me they didn't replay it in slow motion on the national networks.

That January 2nd, 1976 Orange Bowl was the hardest hitting game I have ever been in at any level. We were so young. Our entire offensive line was sophomores or first year starters, the backfield was comprised of a freshman, sophomore, junior and senior, ends and receivers were sophomores and juniors. The defense was similar except a few linebackers and Donny Dufek at wolf. We played Oklahoma (who won the National Championship) straight up and only really had two bad plays. Once we fumbled inside our own 20 that led to an Oklahoma score and another Dan Jelik had Brooks their big receiver dead to rights 10 yards back in the backfield on a reverse. Somehow Brooks slipped the tackle and raced 50 some yards for a score.

Otherwise, it was a tough, tough game. Starting in the fourth quarter Bo went to our "special formation" where we went with 3 wide outs. Keith Johnson would split out to the wide side and Jim Smith would go to the slot. I would split out on the backside and this was our "passing" offense. This had always been a lucky formation in that I usually was the forgotten one when we did this in practice and I usually ran free and had the most success.

I know I did feel lucky. After another incompletion I went to the sidelines. I looked to my left and there was a photographer from the Michigan Daily on the sidelines. She looked directly at me and gave me a big smile. I looked back and winked at her. Hmm, I thought to myself, is it me, am I going to get lucky and change the game here?

The very next play I ran a drag across the middle and was open. Leach fired the ball and it unfortunately sailed well over my head. I was really lucky because I was so exposed up there in the air that Zeke Anderson, the Sooners' safety could have broken me in two! Our luck ran out with the clock and we walked off the Orange Bowl turf with a 14-6 defeat.

Following the game, there was to be an after Bowl party at the Indian Creek Country Club. The Orange Bowl committee had brought in 180 flight attendants to be the escorts for all of the players (Bo was not very happy about that and made sure we all understood that we were to behave like Michigan men). This was also were I first learned how "others" played the game.

At the after Bowl party, for whatever reason the organizers intermixed the teams at tables and I was seated with Tinker Owens, who was an Oklahoma receiver. During the course of the meal he asked me how I did on my tickets. Again, I didn't realize at the time what he was talking about. Tinker was 26 and already had a family to support. He wanted to know how I did on my ticket *sales*. I told him I didn't know what he was talking about as I had given my extra seats away to my teammates who needed tickets. My parents did not fly out for the game as that was a long way from California.

Tinker was astonished. He told me that it was standard operating procedure for Oklahoma to bunch player tickets together and sell them to the highest bidder. Sometimes he could get upwards of $500 per seat. So for a game like the Orange Bowl where he could get 8 seats he could make $4000. Even if he got half that again for the regular season he could support his family on that kind of money.

Needless to say I was blown away. First I never could get my hands on tickets as we could only put names in at will call for people to use the tickets. Secondly, that was absolutely against NCAA regulations. Holy cow, I'd never jeopardize Michigan and its future. Besides all of that it was just plain wrong.

But that sure didn't seem to bother Barry Switzer and Oklahoma. Yes, they have National Championship rings and yes, they won the game on the field, but not my respect. It opened my eyes to how some people view success at the game of football. I knew then that I wouldn't trade my experience at Michigan for all of the rings won under unique circumstances, happy to know the ones I earned would be legitimate.

At the Orange Bowl. Left to right are, Jim Czirr, Curt Stephenson, Kevin King, Jim Hackett, Gerry Szara, and Mark Donohue.

CHAPTER 33
THE DAY AFTER

A number of things happened in the space of 24 hours to me that would impact my final two years as a Wolverine. At the time they had very little significance to the outcome of the Orange Bowl but would change the way my legacy with the University of Michigan would be judged. After our loss to Oklahoma there was a huge party that I have written about where I basically discovered that Oklahoma bought their title and players. After this party I went back to the hotel room and through boredom I went down to the lobby and walked out to the boat docks that surrounded the hotel. There was a big party going on that a lot of players were at on one of the boats.

I strolled down to see what was happening. It was near midnight and we didn't have a curfew as it was after the game. I walked on to the boat and saw that the photographer that I had winked at during the game was on the boat as well. I went up to her and started a conversation. She didn't believe I was from California so I showed her my driver's license. We had a great time and I decided that I was going to try and date this girl when I arrived back in Ann Arbor.

The second thing that happened during the game that I didn't realize would impact me was that Rick White had sprained his knee running an out pattern during the game. What ever the reason, whether it was the sprain or that Rick was also trying to focus on basketball, he determined that he would not participate in spring practice. With Keith Johnson graduating this meant that I would be the only returning letterman at split end for the 1976 season.

It was a very young team. Leach, as a freshman quarterback with Huckleby, Russell Davis, Johnson and Smerge also freshman, Downing, Dufek, Kenn, Donohue, were all sophomore starters on the line. This would be rounded out by Jim Smith and Rob Lytle as the tailback and flanker. The path was there, right in front of me to be the starter at split end. I didn't realize it at the end of the Orange Bowl or the next day, but it dawned on me on the plane ride home on January 4th. If I did what was asked and I performed at my best I could be the starting receiver for the Michigan Wolverines. My dream was unfolding right in front of me.

I wasn't nervous, I wasn't excited. The previous 3 years had prepared me to take this in stride. I had witnessed other upper classmen become leaders on the team and do so with a certain grace, a certain leadership quality that I felt prepared to do so as well. I resolved to lead by example. I would hustle every practice, try to be the first on the field, win every race and show the younger players what it meant to be a starter. Besides, we still had some major work to finish…. we needed to go to the Rose Bowl!

CHAPTER 34
BAND ON THE RUN

It was a bitterly cold day in February 1976. One of my roommates and I were contemplating our futures over breakfast. We were going in opposite directions. I was the only returning letterman at the split end position on a club that everyone knew was going to enter the season as the number one ranked team in the nation. He, on the other hand, had just gotten out of a cast and was hoping that his new job would see him through the year. He had blown his knee out the fall before running down on kick off coverage against MSU.

Back then there weren't lasers and orthoscopic cameras that could get you back on your feet and back into reasonable playing shape in short order. No, he had been sliced open and the procedure was an attempt to staple the ligament to the bone. If successful he would have 75% range of motion and an "S" scar on the inside of his left knee for the rest of his life.

But it was not successful and his playing days were over. He did not take it well. His grades suffered. He drank way too much and got in fights at the local bars for the most ridiculous reasons. (Most were attempts to prove that he was still a hard nosed player). Back then, one thing was for certain. If a Michigan player ran afoul of the law Bo knew about it before the teachers, the students and the school.

My roommate lost his scholarship that year. I couldn't blame him. It was a sad set of circumstances. He still wanted to be treated like an All

American he had been in high school. All of that changed in an instant. What a cruel tragedy. He loved the game and it had made him an idol in his home town. That same game played a horrible hoax on him by taking all of that away and he had spiraled (almost) out of control.

It was hard, but my roommate worked toward righting his ship. He took a job bouncing concerts at Crisler Arena (I don't think that they knew he had been in a cast for four months and one leg was half the size of the other). Most of the players bounced concerts during the summer but with classes and winter conditioning there was no time to do it now. At breakfast, that day he said Paul McCartney and Wings were going to be performing that night, and if I wanted to get into the show he was working the stage. All I had to do was show up about two hours early at the tunnel and he'd open the door and let me in. This was right after the Band on the Run album had come out. I showed up as requested and had been hanging by the door for about ten minutes freezing my butt off.

Right then a limo pulled up, and out pop Paul and Linda McCartney. My roomy magically appears and opens the door for them. Paul turned to me and said," Trying to sneak in are ya, well have a go with these". Then he handed me two front row seats for the show.

Even though my roommate and I looked like our futures were going in opposite directions, for the next four hours we had the same future... front row, singing as loud as we could.

CHAPTER 35
SUMMER JOBS

The mid -70s was really when football started to become a full time occupation for student athletes. Prior to that most guys went home for the summer, but by 1976 it was *clearly* understood that you stayed in Ann Arbor if you wanted to play the following year.

As a result the "summer job program" really had a lot of meaning to most of the guys.

There were lots of jobs to be had and the administration was very good at finding something for one of the guys if he was in real need. But by far and away there were four jobs that were the cream of the crop. They were the most sought after, best paying, and provided great flexibility. These jobs were the General Motors Test Driving jobs.

GM and Ford were always good about getting summer jobs, but most were "on the line". The best of the best were the four slots to road test cars and trucks for GM out at the Midland Proving Grounds. There was also a little exclusivity going on amongst the players. For a few straight years it appeared that only defensive linemen were getting these jobs. I think Jeff Perlinger ("Pearl") handed the job to Greg Morton ("Mo") and he, in turn handed it down to John Hennessy ("Hen"). Anyway, the summer of 1976 I got lucky and was slated for one of the spots.

Mo and Hen were going to show me the ropes. They were going to both graduate the following year so I made sure that the following year the jobs went to receivers (hence in 1977 the jobs went to me, Rick

White, and Max Richardson). The job was the graveyard shift that way you were free during the day to work out. Basically, we were given a car to drive around the proving grounds. There was durability testing where you drove through salt washes, over cobble roads and through dirt and mud. We floored the gas going up hills and rode the brakes going downhill.

The premise was to try and wreck the car without physically getting in an accident. GM wanted to see how much a car could take. Other times we did speed and endurance testing. This was done out on a 4.5 mile oval track. You would race around the track at different speeds so GM could log the mile efficiency, test the tires and engines.

One of the great things a night job offered was I got to listen to all the Detroit Tiger games, especially when they were on road trips to California and the games would go way into the night. That's were I fell in love with George Kell and Ernie Harwell. They were the "voices" of the Tigers and I never heard better announcers. They did everything so smooth and the process was so effortless for those guys. Michigan had a great announcer too, in Bob Ufer. He wasn't like the Tiger announcers though. Ufer was a ball of fire, a hundred miles an hour, and so one sided it made you laugh. He loved his " Meeecheeeegan" and was just like the speed testing at the proving grounds, non-stop, pure excitement. I loved it when he would say," That Gordie Bell could run five minutes in a phone booth and never touch the sides" or "Russell Davis went in there like a bull with a bee in his ear."

Man, back then we had the best of everything.

Back to the proving grounds, where my first day I was immediately abandoned by Mo and Hen and I got stuck with a guy (I can't remember his name) who was going to show me how to speed test. What would be tough about this, after all it was only driving a car! We drove out to the oval track and his job was to run the car at 110 miles an hour for four hours. I figured we'd be bored stiff after an hour.

The track is banked so that if you got up into the outermost lane you were at a 45-degree angle and centrifugal force would hold you in the lane without having to steer. When he got the car into the outside lane and up to 110 miles an hour he put on the cruise control. Imagine my fear when he unbuckled himself, crawled over the seat into the back and proceeded to fall asleep! He calmly said, "Don't worry I'll wake up before four hours."

I almost wet my pants! I told him that the car would surely run out of gas before four hours at 110 mph. His response was, "Well, then we'll just drift down to the center, don't worry kid there is no one out here at 2:00am."

I never fell asleep on that job but I have to admit it ... test-driving was an absolute blast.

CHAPTER 36
DAMN GLOVES

In the 70's we didn't have the indoor football facility that exists today. To tell you the truth, I think Bo didn't want one. He used to love spring practice. It was cold and harsh outside, and he used to holler, "Men, if we're going to fight in the north Atlantic we're going to practice in the north Atlantic!"

There were plenty of terrible things to complain about, especially when it was 10 degrees with the wind blowing and the damn ball felt like you were trying to catch a frozen shot put. I prayed my fingers didn't snap off. But the two worst things for me were stretching and goal line. You had just come out of a warm locker room completely dry and Bo would say "hit it" so we all had to get on the ground for stretching.

Now it wasn't bad if the ground was frozen. What I hated was when it was sleeting and the ground was wet. That cold water went through you like icy razor blades and the old man just loved it. He always had a smile on those days. You've probably heard about the yard stick he'd walk around with to measure splits between the offensive line. Right! Sometimes he just whack you to see if you were paying attention. Like any of us would be falling asleep in the cold!

Yep, he wanted us tough.

Then there was goal line. This was the scrimmage that pitted the first offense against the first defense starting on the 10 yard line going into the end zone. It was pure smash mouth. Now, I was a receiver so I didn't have a lot to do because number one, we *never* threw down near the goal line and number two, there was no where to run. So I couldn't keep warm by running around and the defensive backs knew I wasn't going to catch a pass so they just left us and ran in to try and stop the run. At least the guys on the line could hit each other to get the blood flowing.

It was basically 45 minutes of freezing while most likely being wet. It was worse for the defensive line. In the spring of 1976, mind you, we had a line that was the best in the nation and back then Mo (and Bo) prided on a defensive line made of speed and quickness. Greg Morton didn't weigh any more than 225 pounds, Steve Graves was only 215 pounds, and John Hennessey topped out at 235 pounds. So when Billy Dufek ("Do Rod"), Mike Kenn ("Big Fella"), Mark Donohue ("Paw") and Walt Downing ("Wallllter") started pounding it was no fun for anyone but them and Coach Hanlon. It was a sight to behold and I can still hear the echoes of the pads smashing today.

On one day, it was really nasty outside. Billy D. asked if he could wear gloves. Yep, he had the guts to ask Bo and Hanlon!!! The entire locker room was silent. Guys had tried to wear them before and were screamed at to" get those damn things off". Bo was burning a hole through Billy with his piercing eyes. The whole room was silent as some guys were peaking from behind lockers to witness the carnage; others gladly went to the stalls to miss the outburst.

Billy wasn't about to go quietly. He said, "All you coaches have them on." There was a glint of a laser in Bo's eyes then the scowl turned into a big smile, the laser turned into a twinkle and he started to laugh. He blurted, "Sure, what the hell, they don't do us any good either." Falk then passed out these cotton gloves to everyone but the receivers (Bo wouldn't go that far)... and it turned out that they were like thin gardening gloves. The funny thing was, the gloves got soaked in seconds and were worthless.

It might have been a hollow victory for Billy D. but it was a victory nonetheless.

There is no way on earth to replace those good times.

CHAPTER 37
SPRING FOOTBALL 1976

I eased my way out of my front door on to McKinley. It was less than a two-minute walk to be inside the hallowed halls of the Michigan Football building, even though there was a good two feet of snow everywhere I made it in plenty of time. The cold was harsh and numbing.

Sitting in front of my locker I made sure I put on three pairs of socks. It was still hard to breathe, what with the broken nose I received in the practice the day before. That had been no one's fault. It was one of those things that just happened. Chinstrap pops off and your helmet slides down where the plastic bridge smashes into you.

Today was our third and long scrimmage. What a trip! We were the nation's top option team, one that never threw the ball and we were going to devote a 50-minute scrimmage, in 10-degree weather (wind chill was minus 20) to passing. Trouble was that the defense knew we were going to throw on every play and we had all of 10 passing plays to choose from. So it always was a field day for the defensive backs and a nightmare for the receivers.

I think Bo loved that part the most, to see who would show up and still play with all the odds against you. When I ran out on to the practice turf my hands couldn't clinch, and my nose told me it was going to be a long, painful practice. Even in warm ups catching the ball felt like catching a rock. My head throbbed, my eyes watered, and somehow after 20 minutes my hands began to warm. I said this before, Bo never, ever allowed a receiver to wear gloves.

You gotta love the Winter Wonderland in February. I was wondering what I was doing! Part of me couldn't wait to get over to the Theta house to get warmed up again (after sneaking upstairs). The other part knew I had to prove myself again. Rick White had turned his knee in the Orange Bowl a month earlier and Keith Johnson was graduating. Jim Smith and I were the only guys returning with any game experience and I had a chance to start. Leach hated these scrimmages too because he never looked good. As I said, it was hard to look good when everyone knew you were going to throw and the defensive backs knew all the routes. It was like they were reading our minds.

The only advantage Smith had was he was bigger and stronger than Jim Pickens and Dwight Hicks. My advantage was I was faster than Jerry Zuver and Derek Howard so occasionally we'd sneak a catch in there. Bo called "Red 38 pass". This was a strong formation to the right where Smith split out off the line and Gene Johnson lined up at the TE on that side. Leach would come down the line, fake the option (like anyone would react), and throw to either the TE or Flanker (who ever the safety didn't jump). My job was to split the weak side corner and safety to draw attention.

Here's where it gets good. Everyone knows that Leach is going to throw to Smith so he figures he's going to cross them up and throw deep down the middle to the decoy (me). Well we run the play and the ball gets caught up in the wind and Hicks runs right through my face just as the ball gets there. *Bang!* There is a huge collision and the pass is broken up.

On my way back to the huddle, I can feel my nose start bleeding again and I hear Bo yelling at Leach for the bonehead read. As I bend over Bo says, "I can't believe I found a tough receiver from the creamy beaches of California.......but you should have caught the damn ball". He then called, "81 cross country". This is a play where Smith and Johnson cross each other over the middle at 5 and 15 yards deep and I run as a decoy (what else?) through the safety to occupy him.

Leach drops back cocks his arm and throws deep to me! My eyes are watering, my nose is bleeding, but somehow I catch the thing for a fifty yard touchdown. On the way back to the huddle I hear Bo screaming at the defense, "you sons of bitches thought you knew everything! Quit guessing!"

Back in the huddle, Bo winks at Leach and me and says "Hell, we gotta keep 'em honest". The memory still brings a smile to my face.

CHAPTER 38

COME ON

"Come on", he said, "It'll be a blast!"

My old roommate was trying to get me to perform in a musical rendition of "Sha Na Na". This was something I did my freshman year as a lark. A group of us had bought gold lame jumpsuits and, named ourselves "Frankie and the Fireballs" and performed old tunes from the late '50s and early '60s at Markley Hall. We did this for a dorm sponsored dance and somehow it caught on like wildfire. Other residence halls and sororities hired us to perform at their dances and we even got paid!

We would lip synch tunes of real artists like Jerry Lee Lewis "Great Balls O Fire", "Blue Moon", and "Rock Around the Clock". I did this all through my freshman and first half of my sophomore years. This was when no one knew me on the team, and since my second year was my red shirt year, I wasn't ever recognized. Plus it was a pretty good way to earn some money and meet a lot of girls.

We probably did about 10-12 dances and then we stopped right at the end of 1974. But now he was trying to get me to do an encore performance at the Michigan Union. Our last performance was over a year ago. Now I was the starting receiver on the number one ranked team in the nation. I wasn't seriously considering doing this, was I? My old roomy blurted out, "We're already selling tickets and we've sold over 2000. We get to split the money with the Union so we'll each make about thousand bucks."

Hey, in 1976 a thousand dollars was a lot of money so in March, 1976 I agreed to be "Frankie" one more time. The original outfit was half a topcoat made from gold lame. It had no buttons and was wide open to expose our chests. The girls in the band wore sweaters, poodle skirts and bobbie socks. Our pants were also gold lame. Each of the guys used an entire tube of dippity-doo in our hair to slick it just right, making us quite an oddity to witness.

After practicing for a few weeks we hit the stage at the Michigan Union. There were over 2500 students in the audience and we did our tunes. I'm not sure how many students recognized me but it wasn't very many. Some Michigan football players were in the audience and they were having a blast, laughing their heads off at their ridiculous teammate up on the stage. On the second to last song I tried to do the jump splits in the middle of the stage and I torn my pants in half. That actually was okay because I had something ready for the last song.

I hurriedly went back stage and changed and when I walked out I was wearing chinos with cuffs, white socks, converse all-stars and my Michigan Letterman's jacket. The entire place erupted with wild cheers when I opened the jacket. I had a gray T-shirt that had a very derogatory remark regarding Ohio State (let's just say the last two words were "the Bucks" and it rhymed with what preceded it).

Playing in front of 100,000 fans is an eye opening experience and can be deafening. I would put these 2500 Michigan students up against anyone, anytime. That was the loudest outburst I've ever heard. The place went absolutely mad. There may be some of you out there that won't believe this story. But, a picture is worth a thousand words.

Frankie of Frankie and the Fireballs but "Surf" to his teammates

CHAPTER 39

HOT DAMN

Our 1976 team was in rarified air. We had high aspirations, and it was evident from the first day of camp. Back then, Bo had the entire team tested before we put on pads. I don't know what they do now, but Bo set our routine in stone. Strength coach, Mike Gittleson would throw in some wrinkles, but the old man got a kick out of watching his boys extend themselves. We had a weight that we had to report at, and we had been tested and timed the previous spring and those were benchmarks that we were judged against. Those who didn't make weight they ran at 6:00am ("Dawn Patrol") with Coach Reed and were placed on "Fat man's Table" for all the meals, where caloric intake was highly monitored. In 1976 there were no starters on Fatman's Table, which shows how focused we were.

The tests were strength (military press, bench press, pull ups, and dips); endurance was a 1.5 mile run; speed was sixteen repeat 40 yard sprints (15 seconds rest in between) and we had to run them all within .5 seconds of the fastest time each of us had run in the spring; and finally, agility drills. Points were allotted based upon your times and number of reps. In previous years, Bo had wanted all of his linemen under 250 pounds. He wanted them quick. The first to break that mold was Dan Dierdrof in 1969. I think Dan was born at 270 pounds! But, there was no way Bo could get our line below 250, with the exception of Mike Kenn.

With Dufek, Downing, Donohue and Szara that would be impossible. Our tight ends, Johnson and Smerge were close to 240 pounds.

We were in good spirits when we saw Calvin O'Neal bench 500 pounds with an easy rep, and then he ripped off 35 reps at 225 pounds. When it came time for dips I thought I put up a pretty good number with 50. Trust me there was no cheating. If you didn't go all the way down and lock out at the top you got no credit. Rob Lytle pumped 75, looked around and jumped off. I think he could have done 150!

The sprints were murder. I was a legit 4.5 in the forty so all 16 of mine had to be run under 5 seconds. That may not sound hard, but try 16 in a row with 15 seconds rest and you'll see how difficult it is. Lytle was a 4.4. He popped his first three in 4.4, 4.5, 4.5, and then he ballooned to a 4.9 and was history after that. Robby had these huge thighs and he could explode for bursts but he got thick quickly.

Besides me, there was only a few that made all 16 in the required time. I can't remember my exact time in the 1.5 mile run but I set another Michigan record. Again, I had logged over 1000 miles that summer while I stayed in Ann Arbor averaging 10 to 12 miles a day so I knew I would have no problem with the running.

Finally we got to put pads on, and our first drill set the tone for the year. The seven man sled. This required the center, both guards, tackles, the tight end and the split end to hit the sled. Remember we were an option team so we all hit the sled.

Bo put six coaches on the sled for extra weight. We lined up, me, Kenn, Szara, Downing, Donohue, Dufek and Johnson. When we fired out there was such an explosion, the sled rose five feet in the air and all the coaches fell off. The whole team broke out laughing.

Bo looked over and muttered, "Hot damn."

We knew we had a team.

CHAPTER 40
ORDINARY MAN

Heading into the 1976 season Bo had recently undergone major bypass surgery. We all knew that he had previously suffered a heart attack just before the Rose Bowl in 1969, so there was a lot of concern regarding his health. During the summer months we watched him as he started his routine to try to get back on the field. I remember him struggling to run one lap around the football field. He had started by walking and worked his way up to jogging.

Though we were concerned about our coach, we were in high spirits. We were about to start hitting and the days would be long and hot through the third week in August. We came out for our first full padded practice for double sessions and all the receivers and backs began to stretch and loosen up. The way we did this was to form two lines at the opposite ends of half the field. One line would form on the goal line and the other would form at the opposite end starting at the fifty. Guys would jog five to eight yards and the quarterbacks would flip the ball to you and you'd run down to the other end to hand it to an equipment guy who would give it to another quarterback and start the whole process over.

After about 10 or 12 passes the quarterbacks would start to lengthen their throws. Pretty soon they were throwing the ball 25 to 30 yards downfield. When the length of the throws expanded the width of the routes the receivers would run expanded as well. Bo would normally stand right on the fifty and watch the proceedings, every now and then giving a tip to a quarterback (either telling him to get more air under his throws, or to keep the ball within a few feet of the sideline so as to not let the receiver drift out of bounds).

However on this day, Bo, new arteries and all, had his back to the proceedings, as the trainers were checking him out. Soon, the throws were exceeding fifty yards in length. We called these "nine" routes or "Flies" or "take offs". All we did, basically was run as fast as you could down the field. The quarterbacks in the meantime were trying to air their arms out and they repeated threw the ball higher and farther than normal. This was a tricky catch because most times you were looking over one shoulder, trying to stay in bounds and a lot of the time the ball would be coming down right over the top of you head or your opposite shoulder. Either way, you were never looking at what was in front of you.

I had just caught a long pass and I was watching a young receiver, Mike Harden, take off from the end zone running out toward the fifty. The quarterback, Stacey Johnson, really let it out and the ball was sailing way out of bounds toward the training area. Harden –fully padded, mind you- drifted to his right and tracked the ball. He never even saw Bo and ran him right over. Bo went down head first, then rolled into a huge ball with Mike right on top of him. It was a nasty collision, and we feared the worst.

Amazingly, Bo sprang to his feet and announced to the whole team, "Gentlemen, that would have killed an ordinary man". The whole place burst out into laughter. Even if the old man was exaggerating a little bit, we all knew he was not ordinary.

CHAPTER 41

VINTAGE BO

It was late August 1976 and the team had been hitting for almost two weeks through double sessions. Typical summer days in Ann Arbor would run into the low to mid 90's, which meant it was about 120 degrees inside your helmet. The rubber backing on the tartan turf would absorb the heat and in the afternoon practice the turf would project up heat that was well in excess of 100 degrees. Heat exhaustion was always a worry for Lindsey McLean, our trainer.

It had only been the last few years where coaches were now convinced that water was good to take prior, during and after practice. Just a few years earlier, the common practice was to deprive yourself of water in an effort to make you tough. Now, Bo gave us water breaks. We had these pump canisters that would shoot out a stream of water so that you could fire it between your facemask without taking off your helmet. Most guys would get a good swig and then douse their necks so the cool water would run down your back under your pads.

This particular day was a little different. Huge storm clouds rolled in right after the morning practice and there was a general "tornado watch". Bo didn't care. We had work to do and we were damn sure going to get that work done. Leach had been on the cover of *Sports Illustrated*. We were touted as the number one team in the country. We knew we were good, too. From the early lifting and hitting we could tell this was a special team. Bo knew it and wanted us to work that much harder, but we had fun as well.

As we were dressing for the afternoon practice we could hear huge cracks of thunder outside. I hadn't experienced thunder and lighting like this in California. Sure, we had earthquakes to deal with but it never seemed to be this bad! It was dark as night when we took the field. I actually liked it, because the temperature must have dropped into the 70's. The rain was surely going to cool everything off, tartan surface and all. Right when we started to scrimmage bright cracks of lighting looked like they were splitting portions of Ferry Field. These bolts were only where only a few hundred yards away.

Kirk Lewis, our Captain, began to protest to Bo that anyone of the players could be hit by lighting. Bo immediately retorted, "Mr. Lewis, we all know how intelligent you are as you're studying to be a doctor. We would have thought you knew that all of you players are wearing rubber-soled cleats. There are no metal cleats out here on out turf, therefore you are all grounded and the electricity will pass right through you."

Lewis replied, "Coach, you are correct that we are wearing rubber soled cleats, but all the linemen are putting their bare hands on the turf and therefore ungrounded." At this Bo laughed and asked Hanlon why Lewis was so smart. He turned back to our captain and said, "Duly noted, point well taken, now get in the damn huddle!"

This was all done with that Schembechler smile that said so many different things....something like, "okay smart ass you got me", or "aren't we having fun out here?" Either way, when we saw that smile, we all knew we were safe, we knew we were good and we knew we were preparing to be the best.

CHAPTER 42

WISDOM TEETH

Right before the start of the season in 1976 I had to have my wisdom teeth extracted. This was problematic for a number of reasons. First, I needed all four out at the same time and the bottom two teeth were impacted. As I was told when this is the case most dentists prefer to put the patient completely out. My problem was that for me to be put out completely I would have to miss practice. If I missed practice then I wouldn't be able to play in the game (Bo's rules). Meaning there was no way I was going to miss practice regardless of the pain in my mouth.

I spent the day trying to get the team dentist to fit me in on a Sunday in between patients he was seeing so I could avoid all the issues. He kept telling me I was crazy, as I would be missing practice on Monday and Tuesday anyway to recover from the surgery. He underestimated my need to play and my desire to help the team win another game. There was *no way* I was going to miss a practice. He finally indicated that there was no way he could fit me in as he was fully booked but he did have a suggestion. He told me to go to the dental school and have the procedure done by a dental student (sort of like practice).

He knew they could get me in late Monday and maybe, just maybe I could make it to a Tuesday practice. In addition, all I'd only have to pay $50 per tooth. I decided to take this route. I scheduled the procedure through the dental school for the next Monday. I also told them that I refused to have general anesthesia.

The procedure ended up as a, good news, bad news story. The lower two impacted teeth had to be cut and broken in two to be extracted. To do this, the student dentist injected Novocain into my lower jaw on both the right and left side. He also injected Novocain on my upper right side, and then he ran out of "juice". As I was numbing, he left and came back and started to work on the lower jaw.

The first two teeth took about 10 minutes each to extract. He then put a special tool on the upper right tooth and it seemed to be pulled as if it was coming out of butter. At this point I was in a fog. When he put the tool on the other tooth I expected him to shoot me with Novocain there, but he must have forgot he hadn't and immediately pulled the tooth! This was one of the most painful things I have ever endured. Blood gushed from the wound and I ripped the upholstery of the chair I was sitting in.

All at once, all hell broke loose. The dental student realized what he had done and was at a loss to do anything. I was so fortunate that Tom Slade was on the floor at the time. Tom had been the starting quarterback in 1972 before losing his starting job in 1973 to Dennis Franklin (my freshman year). Tom had gone to dental school immediately after graduating and was "in residence" at my unfortunate incident. He quickly calmed everyone and took control of the situation.

I was told I didn't have to pay anything (yeah, right!). Tom told me that the kid who did my surgery would never forget what happened and would probably make a great dentist one day. He told me that there was no way I would be practicing on Tuesday and he'd make sure I got home. He'd also call Bo and tell him what happened and put in a good word for me.

I went home that afternoon and I looked like a chipmunk. My cheeks were swollen and I had to ice them down. Around 1:00 pm Tuesday I got a call from Lynn (Bo's assistant). She said that Tom had called and gave Bo the entire story. What Bo had told him in response was that Tuesday is a heavy work day (we scrimmage) and if he (meaning me) chose to have his teeth pulled and he misses practice, tough, he misses the game.

Upon hearing this, I got up off the couch and headed off to practice. I had gauze crammed into my mouth and I couldn't stop drooling. As Bo said, Tuesday was a heavy hitting day. My face was so swollen that

I couldn't put a mouth guard in my mouth. When I leaned over in the huddle, I couldn't stop the spit and blood mixture from drooling down and hanging on my facemask. It got to the point where Jim Smith and Rob Lytle wouldn't even form up in the huddle.

After awhile, Bo finally conceded and yelled, "Stephenson, get out of the damn huddle. We need to get some work done." I was only too happy to comply, as I needed to get some aspirin fast. We did get our work done and beat Wisconsin, 40-27. Oh, and I did get to start that game.

CHAPTER 43
GERRY, WALT AND ME

We started the 1976 season off great and kept rolling. We were ranked number one by everyone. We caused opposing coaches to lie awake at night worrying about their next job. Leach was running the show, and he had weapons galore. His line was wall-to-wall All Americans (Dufek, Donohue, Downing and Kenn). The fullback was Russell Davis with Rob Lytle at tailback. Then we'd move Lytle to fullback and bring in Harlan Huckleby. Jim Smith held the wingback position and yours truly was the split end (not saying that I was a weapon).

We were told that we would have a special visitor on Wednesday's practice; none other than the President of the United States, Gerald Ford, who was a former Wolverine himself. He was going to be in the area, and I guess he wanted to drop by and see the team. Practice went as planned, but half way through there was a big commotion. Secret service agents flowed on to the field and then the President appeared.

He walked right out to Bo, and they shook hands. Bo immediately spun around and hollered, "you'll all get to meet him after you finish your work." President Ford stood right by our huddle as we were preparing our offense to face Stanford. One of Bo's favorite plays was the "Sally", nicknamed after the famous stripper "Sally Rand". The play got this name because it was a naked reverse. Bo yelled out the play "Red Special, Sally". I ran out to my wide position on the far right with Smith in the slot.

The second and third teams had moved back because, they all knew it would be a fake sweep to Lytle and a pitch back to Smith reversing deep behind the line of scrimmage. Bo moved back with them but the President hadn't moved at all. Right at the snap Bo barked to President Ford, "You'd better get back", just as Smith blew by him. Smitty came within inches of running over the most powerful man on the face of the earth!

The President's face lit up, and you could see the rush in his face as the whole team blew by him. It seemed as though the memories of his playing days came back to him, because he lit up with such a smile. Later he addressed the team in the locker room and gave us encouragement to beat Stanford. We obliged him with a 51-0 win.

Bo invited the President to our training table, which sort of turned it into a zoo. The secret service agents had to check every player before we were allowed to enter. We gathered our food and sat down at the tables. I was sitting right next to Walt Downing (our All American center). When the President entered he requested to sit next to Michigan's center, as Mr. Ford had played that same position. So the President plops down right between Walt and me. He was very cordial and shook hands with everyone.

A tray appeared with a big New York steak in front of the President. Walt was busy on his second when the President dug into his. What happened next was kind of a blur.

President Ford started to choke and the secret service started to circle the table. I don't know why, but in one immediate action, I reached back and gave him a good whack on the back. A hunk of beef flew out and across the table. The President turned to me and said "Thanks".

Others weren't as grateful. From that point on, there were about six agents who were giving me eagle eyes. But we all had a good laugh over that one, Gerry, Walt and me.

CHAPTER 44

FIRST CATCH

In 1976, we were getting more exposure that a Michigan had received in decades and certainly more than any other Schembechler team in the past. Bo absolutely hated this. He wanted no part of the press, and he certainly didn't want any of his players talking to them without his complete control.

This was also my first year to catch a pass. I wasn't called a wide receiver back then, in fact I was referred to as a wide guard by my family and friends, mainly because 90 percent of the time I blocked for our option play and the other 10 percent I ran as a decoy so we could throw the ball to Jim Smith or our tight ends.

Keith Johnson, who was the split end before me never caught a pass his junior or senior year. Think about that, a wide receiver at a major division one university not catching a pass in two years! This begs the question, "How in the world could Michigan convince Anthony Carter to come there knowing the split end position had caught ten passes in the previous five years? Tells you how good a recruiter Bo was!

About, the only great thing about being a wide guard for Michigan in the mid 70's was if they threw to you (and that was a huge if) you were so wide open it was laughable (case in point and trivia time: guess what my yards per catch average was for my career)?

Would you believe it was over *41 yards per catch?*. Regardless of my limited use in the passing game, we were blowing people out and winning big. We had at least six backs that were averaging over 5.5 yards per carry and everyone was getting playing time.

Leach had thrown an out to me early against Illinois and I caught it but was ruled out of bounds on the sideline. Heading into the game with Northwestern, who we had spanked the year before 69-0, I wasn't figuring on playing too long. In the second quarter at mid- field, Gerry Szara brought in a play, "White special 39 pass". I was shocked. The play wasn't to me as I was the third read but what shocked me was that we were throwing the ball so early in the game. I think we were up 14-0 at the time and moving at will even though Northwestern was putting eight to nine in the box to try and stop the option.

I split out to the left sideline and ran a "nine" route. This is a fly pattern as fast as you can go. Leach faked the ball to Russell Davis through the three hole, and Lytle swung out wide for the option pitch. As soon as Leach got to the end he backed up three steps and was to hit Smith running a seam route down the hash. The play didn't go as planned and ended up being my good fortune. Both the safety and linebacker, reading option, flew to the line of scrimmage and right in the path of the throw to Smitty. This also meant that no one was deep with me.

The cornerback also jumped the option and when Rick threw the ball I was ten yards behind the corner. I caught it at about the 15- yard line and was immediately hit by the back side safety and went out of bounds around the 10- yard line. We scored two plays later, but I still took grief. It wasn't because I should have scored; it was because it was my first catch in almost 20 games!

Jon Falk asked if I wanted the ball for a keepsake, muttering something like, "maybe we should bronze it." Mike Kenn wanted me to autograph it so he could actually say he knew a split end at Michigan with a catch. Bo told me not to get a big head because, "you won't see the ball for another 20 games!"

I might have believed him, too, but that first one certainly felt good.

CHAPTER 45

INDIANA

We were still No.1 in the country when we went down to play Indiana in 1976 in what was a veritable monsoon. Fortunately, we had who Bo had declared the best "wet ball" quarterback he'd ever seen in Rick Leach. Bo had made that statement was because through 1975 and half of the 1976 season Michigan had practiced or played in more rain games than anyone would like to remember.

The past summer had been a blessing for the team in a strange way. Usually during double sessions Bo loved hot weather. He wanted us to prepare in the most strenuous situation possible and 95 degrees with 90% humidity was just the ticket. Strangely, the team only faced one or two days like that the summer before the season. Most of the double sessions of 1976 were held on overcast days with rare summer showers.

There were two results of these types of practices. The first was that it made our team very good at playing in wet weather. The second was the players loved the rain. It provided a reprieve from the unbearable hot days and generally put us in a better mood. It sounds strange but we actually looked forward to a nice cool rain.

When we landed in Bloomington, Indiana the forecast was for showers. All the local papers were focused on the premise that the potential wet weather and wet surface would slow down the powerful Michigan option attack. When we took the field for warm ups there was a light drizzle. By the time we were in full stretching it was a heavy rain. The fans in the stands had three choices. They could scurry up the

109

aisles to try and get under the overhang or they could don umbrellas or slickers. Their final choice was to simply leave.

Many choose to stay and as the umbrellas popped up it began to pour. It was one of the hardest rains I've ever seen. When we saw the Indiana team in their tunnel waiting to come out we found it amusing in that it appeared as if they were reluctant to take the filed. Billy Dufek started a cheer while we were still in full stretch, chanting, "More rain, more rain", challenging the heavens to produce more than the deluge that was showering us already. Soon the whole team was chanting, " more rain, more rain, more rain."

It seemed that we got our wish and it came down in buckets. As it rained harder the Michigan team grew louder with their chants, "more rain, more rain." We broke into our specialty groups and our coaches were laughing as our cheers continued in these drills. Indiana still had not come out yet of their tunnel. It became obvious to any close observer that this band of Wolverines was, in fact, a bunch of lunatics, and we wanted more.

The rain continued until our third series. We were ripping off huge gains and on a play called "Red 38"; Leach gave a perfect pitch to Lytle right at the line of scrimmage. Rob headed downfield but the strong safety had the angle on him. The safety threw everything he had at Robbie. After a huge collision, Lytle, sure footed as ever, did a full 360 degree spin and out raced everyone to the end zone. It was clearly obvious that all the Wolverines had their bearings and Indiana was completely out of place. Maybe it was the rain, who knows but we loved it! Even though we were on the road, we posted an easy win 35-0.

There was one point in the game where Jim Smith and I were throwing cut blocks, not so much to knock down the Indiana defender as to see how many yards we could slide on the soaked astroturf. That was an absolute blast. To this day, I know the Indiana players thought we were all crazy, and so did their fans, but it didn't matter. We, simply, loved wet weather and nobody was going to spoil our fun.

CHAPTER 46
REGULAR DAY

It was a regular day. Now wait a minute.....what's regular? Tuesday afternoon, just before 3:00 pm we would head out to the tartan practice field behind the ten-foot high brick walls that housed the University of Michigan Football team. It sure seemed like it was another regular day.

Did I mention it was Ohio State week? The specialists were lining up to run patterns and loosen the legs. The quarterbacks were beginning to throw easy passes to all the backs and receivers. Over on the sideline there were about six or seven little kids watching the practice. Most were coach's kids with maybe one or two real lucky grade school chums that happened to get the "OK" to tag along with a coach's son to watch the mighty Michigan Wolverines get ready for OSU. Bo was all business. He did have a smile on, but you could see in his eyes there was going to be some heavy work done today.

Tuesday, game week, that was a hitting day. It was a goal line day. That was where our bread was buttered. If we could score a touchdown every time we were down in goal line territory we were going to win. There was work to do and Bo knew how to get the work done, on time, and in the proper way.

It was a regular day for football, but there was something in the air. You could feel it. Everyone sensed it. A win and we were Rose Bowl bound. A win and we chalk up another Championship in the Wolverine annals of history. We all knew that this meant that it would be a lively practice. As Bo would tell it, "Men, today we need to work and I expect it to be spirited." This really meant that he wanted to see some very, very heavy hitting going on.

When we broke into the 7 on 7 drills I guess all the coaches kids got too wrapped up in what was going on and tried to mimic what was happening on the field. There was an apron near the south end of the field that the linemen used for their drills. It was far enough away from the main field that they wouldn't interrupt any drills that were being run on the regular field. Frankly, it was the perfect size for a pick up football game and since the linemen were at the opposite end of the main field getting ready for goal line that's what happened.

A small pick up football game with the kids broke out. They were playing with one of those footballs you got from the Detroit Lions on ball day, plastic, one fifth of the regular size. Most adults couldn't throw a spiral with one, but the little kids were used to them and could fantasize about throwing touchdowns in Michigan Stadium one day. Well, one got away and it bounced right into our drill and a little kid came over to retrieve it. The drill stopped and I was slightly amused, because I knew that the kid would get a real close up experience with Bo himself. But it didn't happen. The kid picked up the ball and ran back to his game. We all looked at the old man, who was shaking his head. All he said was, "Damn, can you believe that!" We resumed practice and the hitting was right at a level that pleased the old man. It was very spirited and rough.

The linemen joined us for goal line when our 7 on 7 drills ended. Now this was a break for me as we never threw down near the goal line. That meant my day was easing down. I looked over at the pick up game, which now had moved on to the main field at about the 40-yard line. I could see one of the kids had on a Leach jersey, number 7, another had on a Jim Smith jersey, number 37 and another had on Rob Lytle's number 41. I wondered to myself if anyone would one day wear a number 85 and try to score imaginary touchdowns as a wide receiver.

The pick up game ran a play. The little kid that had retrieved the ball was running in circles trying to get away from rushers. He cut one way then another and finally heaved the ball.......right into our drill, *again*!

That was it. We all knew something had to happen. Sure enough Bo started, "Damnit, Jack, I'm going to kill that kid of yours!" I have never seen Jack Harbaugh run as fast but he sprinted over and grabbed his youngest son by the collar and led him out off the field and we could hear his son as he was dragged away, "But, Dad, he was wide open!" As they left the field Bo hollered after them, "You tell Jimmy he is never to set foot on the Michigan field again!"

Everyone started laughing even though we were sore. We had been hitting hard all day and our work was almost done. Bo must have been in a great mood because he let that kid, little Jimmy Harbaugh, back on to the field the next day. All was forgiven. In fact that kid stepped on the field many more times.

All this was just another regular day with the Michigan Wolverines, the week before we played Ohio State.

CHAPTER 47

NO BELLS

It had been a good week of practice. We felt good about everything. When we boarded the chartered plane at Detroit Metro and there were a thousand fans at the gates yelling encouragement.

A lot had been going through my mind the past week. Bo didn't have to remind us. It was all on the line now. The Big Ten Championship and a trip to the Rose Bowl were to go to the winner. It was like this every year.

We knew we had to take this one more step. A lot of these guys were on the 1973 team that won a Big Ten Championship but got "voted" out of the Rose Bowl. A lot of the guys were also from the 1974 team that also won a Big Ten Championship, but again were left out of a Bowl game. All the sophomores were on the team that lost to OSU in the last 9 minutes and ended up at the Orange Bowl. We needed to do this for all of those teams and all the other great Michigan teams throughout the years that had come up short in Columbus.

Certain things are funny between these Universities. We had heard stories about Woody showing film of Michigan "cheap shots" to his players to get them fired up. We didn't need anything more than the three years of agony and getting short changed to stoke our fire. Funny how our hotel didn't have hot water from the time we checked in until the time we checked out. It was all part of "The Game".

We were prepared. Our Friday walk through went very well and we all knew something special was going to happen. Big Bill Dufek had been preaching the whole week, "There will be no bells in Columbus".

Those of us who were on the 1974 team, where we prevented OSU from scoring a touchdown and still lost 12-10 on four field goals, knew what he meant. There were these huge bell towers that started ringing the second the game ended. We could even hear them in the locker room and they were still ringing after we had showered and were on our way to the bus.

Billy D. was telling all of us that we had a job to do and that job was to make sure those bells weren't heard this year. Bo had a few tricks up his sleeve, too (Yep, even the old man was going to pull out the stops for this one). We had preplanned on our first offensive possession we would go no huddle and immediately run a 15 yard hook to me.

If you watch a rerun of the game film, on the first play, we do exactly that, problem was that Leach never got the pass off and ended up scrambling.

I wasn't nervous the night before and I slept like a baby. The next morning, I got up and went to the suite that was set aside for training room and tapping. I had them tape my ankles extra tight. OSU had synthetic turf in 1974, which was fake plastic blades of grass, Michigan had tartan turf. The difference was that tartan turf was made up of fine fibers like wires and it grabbed your cleats. The turf was actually fake plastic blades of grass and could get slippery and didn't grab as tight. OSU had gone to a new tartan turf the year before and I didn't want to risk a sprained ankle. Warm ups went by fast and I could tell we were all focused. It was a real high to be at that level when you knew the outcome even before it happened.

The first half was a huge struggle. The OSU punter was their best offense as he was booming punts. We had Jim Smith returning them, and Smitty was ripping off 15-20 yards on each return, putting huge pressure back on Ohio State. I was excited when, late in the second quarter, Bo called a deep pass to me. I knew I could run by their corner back and did so, on the play. Again, if you ever watch this on replay you'll see me running down the sidelines and I trip over the side judge. Heavens knows why, he was in the field of play. He shouldn't have been. In the end Leach attempted something like eight passes the whole game and completed none to Michigan players. That really didn't matter. We still had Smitty returning punts, our big line pounding out first downs, Lytle slashing and our defense playing stone cold shut out football.

The second half was magical. We took the opening kick off and hit Ohio State like a jack hammer. Lytle outside, and Davis inside. We went 80 yards on our first drive with Davis going in from the 3yard line for a 7-0 lead.

Billy D. kept chanting in the huddle "no bells, no bells". After the kick off our defense throttled the Buckeyes and they had to punt from deep in their own territory. I think we got the ball out around our 40.

Again, we asked Kenn, Lewis, Downing, Donohue and Dufek to pound away. We busted out another first down. This series was to be our "change up". You know that both OSU and Michigan ran the same offense (option football) so each team basically knew what the other team was doing, so it really came down three things. Execution, power and subtle changes were the important aspects of the game. Our power was starting to show and with subtle changes we began to rip off some big plays.

The first subtle change was when we ran a "Red Special 38". This was a standard option that was run to the wide side of the field. "Special" meant that I split out to the right and Jim Smith was in the slot with no tight end to our side. When we ran the option like this Smitty would loop and block the safety and I would block the defensive back right in front of me. We were right at midfield and coming out of the huddle Smitty told me to "cross". This meant he would loop like he normally would, but after a few yards he'd turn and kick out the DB on my side. At the same time, I'd release, but then get to crack block on the safety from a "blind" angle to him. It worked to perfection. Smith kicked out the DB and I walled the safety. Lytle took the pitch and rumbled for almost a 20 yard gain.

Two more plays and we were in side the 25 yard line. Then we jumped offside and were moved back to the 30. Now, it was Bo's turn to "change up". He called "Red Special 38 Sally". This was the same play where Rob Lytle had gained almost 20 yards before but instead of pitching to Rob to the right, Leach would pitch and Smitty running a reverse would take the pitch around left end. Smith broke free and ran all the way down to around the 10 yard line.

We punched it in again in a few more plays. Again, Bo did the unthinkable and faked the extra point. Jerry Zuver picked up the snap and could've throw to Lytle in the flat or run it in. He did the latter, and we broke out on top 15-0. The rest of the game was magical.

Mid way through the 4th quarter, we were on cloud nine. It was second down and three from the Buckeye forty. We had been smashing into OSU for eight plays and were averaging six yards per crack. We hadn't attempted a pass in 30 plays and everyone (and I mean everyone) knew the outcome. We were going in again, and there wasn't anything Ohio State could do but take it.

Big Walt Downing bent over the ball and Leach grunted, "Hit" and our massive line exploded into them again. Rick spun, as Russell Davis literally "blew up" the Buckeye linebacker trying to fill the hole and Lytle took the ball and slipped by for another 7 yard gain. As they moved the chains, we were in no hurry. This was the time to savor it. This was the time to remember the past players who had fought so hard and come up short in the horseshoe. Looking around the huddle there was ear to ear smiles on every player.

The rush was amazing. It was so great. Time stood still. I couldn't tell you if it was cool or cold on that November day. Everything seemed to be the right temperature. My helmet didn't hurt like it normally did; the tape around my ankles didn't pinch too hard and the ripped open scabs from landing on Buckeye astroturf didn't hurt. Somebody in the huddle blurted out, "Hey, say hi to Snoopy" as the Goodyear blimp passed overhead. We all looked up and started to laugh.

As we approached the scrimmage line our entire team was chanting "No bells, no bells, no bells". This was one of the greatest thrills of my life. The next play, Rob busted in for our final touchdown. We went on to win 22-0.

OSU was prevented from setting an NCAA record for going the longest without being shut out. My guess was that they would have to start that streak over. As the few Michigan faithful ran on the field, I remember seeing my girlfriend running toward me. She jumped towards me and I forgot that I was still wearing my helmet and I damn near knocked her out.

Walking off that field it was totally quiet, except our Michigan team celebrating. We sang the Victors in the locker room and I remember strolling out to our bus and the entire town of Columbus was silent. It was if they had boarded up the place. I loved every second of it. There were no sounds, no bells, not anything. It was awesome! That was one of those rare times were silence was the greatest noise in the world!

CHAPTER 48
GAME WEEK

We would start on Monday and go through the scouting report of the next week's opponent. The report carried all sorts of information like statistics on each player including their heights, weights, speed and any special interests the coaching staff would like to point out. We would go through their formations and tendencies and Bo was always known to point out one or two of their exceptional players. He was always good for some comment along the lines of, "That Kirk Gibson is the toughest and best receiver in our conference. We probably don't have anyone on our squad who can cover him. Is that right Mr. Hicks?" To which Dwight would propose that he would personally kick Gibson's butt all over the field (which he did by the way).

After this, we would view the latest film on our opponent. Then we'd head out to the field for a very light practice in sweats. We began with standard stretching, then "individuals". This was where we broke into individual groups (quarterbacks, backs, receivers, linebackers, defensive backs and offensive and defensive lines, respectively).

Later we would reform into complete offense and defense units. Our offense would run through the base plays we were going to run the next week and the defense would set up how they were going to attack the other team. This usually would last about 45 minutes and then it was time for our run.

I've mentioned this before, where we would run around cones that would spell the first letter of the team we were going to play. If we were playing Michigan State University we'd run the big "S" for State. These runs, lasted anywhere from 25 to 40 minutes depending on Bo's mood.

After my redshirt year, I always led these runs. This was my sanctuary, knowing I was leading the team, knowing this was a strong suit of mine. I'd holler out encouragement to some of the stragglers, but I would always sprint the last lap so everyone knew we were finished with the run.

Afterward, sometimes I hang around and catch a few balls thrown to me and sometimes I head right to the showers.

Tuesdays were hard practices. We would hit all practice Tuesday. This was full pads and we would run through our offense for over an hour. The defense would be doing the same thing on the other side of the field. In addition, to this we would go through extra point, field goal, goal line and perimeter (which pitted all the skill positions against each other). Perimeter was always fun because we would line up with the two running backs, the quarterback, a tight end and two wide outs against the linebackers and defensive backs. We would then run short passes, intermediate passes, long passes and screens against the defense. This was all done before full offense and full defense, which were the last drills of practice.

Wednesday was the same, only more intense. This practice was full hitting again. When I was on the scout teams, I hated these practices because you usually got the snot kicked out of you for two hours. When I was a regular, up with the first team, these were still hard practices, but you really could take advantage of the scout players.

Dave Brown and Donny Dufek always wanted the scout player to come full steam at them to give them a good look. This was very hard to do when you were getting the s--- kicked out of you on every play. I do know that some guys had "deals" with the scout players to go "easy" on certain plays. If the scout player didn't go easy, then the first teamer would usually kick his butt on the next play.

Then there was always a younger guy wanting to show his stuff and he'd go full blast no matter the circumstances. These little battles were always fun to watch. Bo knew that these were going on all the time and he'd judge guys by how they reacted to the "peer" pressure or the "coach's" pressure. It was always the game within the game, but it brought out those who loved the competition and the game.

Thursday was the day that we ran through the entire game plan. We would run through the entire kicking game, punts, kick offs, field goal and extra point. We would run through goal line and the two minute drill. The hitting was about 75% of what it was on Tuesday and Wednesday.

I will tell anyone who will listen that our practices were way, way harder than the actual games. If you made it through Bo's practices the games were a walk in the park. That was truly a confidence builder. As a player, you knew you were going up against players that were better than the ones you'd face on Saturday. You knew that you were hitting harder than what the hitting would be like on Saturday. By the end of the week, you were looking forward to playing the game. This may sound strange, but I loved Bo for that aspect alone. He made us confident. He made us tough. He made the Saturday game easier than practice. Just think about that. If every challenge that you were going to be judged on you had already gone through and the preparation for that challenge was tougher than the challenge itself, imagine the results.

Fridays were great. These were some of my best memories. If it was a home game we would meet at the Big House around 3:00pm. We would get taped and dressed in the locker room just like we would before the actual game. We would run through the tunnel and out on to that beautiful tartan field. We were only in sweats but the goose bumps would still be there.

After stretching and individuals we'd run field goal. At the very end Bo would always take over for one play down near the goal line. He'd send Leach to the sideline and Bo would play quarterback. Damn, we all loved this! He would call the goofiest plays. The defense would be hooting and hollering, telling Bo they were going to sack him or "kill" him. Bo would take charge of the offensive huddle. He would make a play up. It was always a double reserve pass or unbalanced line, some crazy play that no one had ever practiced. These were the kind of plays that you made up in the back yard when you were playing with your buddies and we loved every second.

Every time we did this Bo would line up under center and bark out the signals. For about ten seconds the defense would act as if they were trying their hardest and right at the crucial moment, whether it was a pass to an eligible tackle, or a naked reverse where Bo ran the ball in to the end zone, somehow the defense would fail and Bo would score.

The team always went crazy and we loved to see the old man do his "touchdown dance" in the end zone. He always had the biggest smile on his face. Man, oh, man those were good times. They were some of the greatest highs watching Bo celebrate, just like we knew we would be doing in less than 24 hours on the same field.

After practice, we would all board the bus to the Campus Inn for home games. On the away games we usually met at the football building and took a bus to the airport for a private charter and we would run through practice that Friday on the opponent's field. However, at home, we would get to the Campus Inn around 6:00pm. We'd then have a full team dinner. These were always the same. The meal consisted of a steak and lasagna with some potatoes and vegetables. The dessert would be a single scoop of vanilla ice cream with chocolate sauce on top.

After dinner, we would all run up to our rooms to gather as many pillows as possible because we would all meet in a big conference room for the "team movie". This was a blast!

Bo usually let the captains in on the selection of the movie, but he always had veto power. Bo loved the action movies. I can't tell you how many times we saw "Dirty Harry" or his personal favorite "Patton", but it was a lot. Once, when we were watching "Blazing Saddles" and when a certain scene came on around the camp fire, our offensive line was bound and determined to out do the actors. We never saw the end of the movie because the room had to be evacuated! We almost died laughing. The coaches were laughing so hard they all had to leave the room.

After the movie we would get a soda, cookie, and an apple for a bedtime snack. It was usually lights out by 11:00pm. We received a visit from your position coach around 10:45pm. In this meeting, you would go over stuff that you had already covered during the week.

My position coach was Tirrell Burton. I knew he was confident that I was smart and knew what I had to do so our meetings were short. Then Bo would come by right at 11:00pm to make sure you were all right. In all my years of bed checks, I don't think he and I had any more to say to each other than, "Stephenson, you OK?" My response, was always, "Yes, sir".

From my junior year on, I always had a single room. I never roomed with anyone else on the team at the Campus Inn. On the road, I roomed with Rob Lytle my junior year, and Rick White my senior year. Saturday morning, game day, was heaven for me in Ann Arbor from 1975 through 1977. I would get up at 7:00am and look out the window. I usually could see all of Ann Arbor to the east from the top floor at the Campus Inn. I loved to see the trees changing colors.

After looking out the windows, I would hustle down the back steps one floor down and get my ankles taped in one of the training rooms. Lindsey McLain and Lenny Paddock never taped me even though they were the two longest reigning trainers. They always taped too loose. I wanted my ankles to be like casts. I wanted a full roll of tape on each ankle. I wasn't going to risk a sprained ankle to keep me from playing and with that much tape on it would require a broken ankle to bust the tape job I'd require. Once that was completed, I went back to my room to sit and ponder the game.

I usually had about an hour before breakfast. We didn't have cell phones and I had no one to call anyway, so I would sit back, flip on the tube (you'll get a kick out of this but at 8:00am in 1976 in Ann Arbor, Michigan, I use to watch old black and white Tarzan movies!) I half heartedly watched them. Mostly my mind was wandering with thoughts , would I catch a pass, would I score a touchdown, how many times would I knockdown the defensive back to allow for a long Michigan run? We'd usually meet around 9:00am and go down for breakfast, after this, it was on to the bus with a full police escort to the Big House.

We took two buses to the stadium. The offense was always on the first bus and the defense was on the second. Bo always road with the offense and he would go over last minute assignments with the starting quarterback. Once we got to the stadium, we would enter our private locker and prepare for the game. I cannot do justice with words and describe getting dressed and running out in front of 100,000 fans. It is a feeling that is only felt by Michigan Football players. In my opinion this is the greatest feeling that an 18-21 year old can experience in their life. I wish you all could experience it. I never want to forget it.

CHAPTER 49

GAME DAY

There mornings were special for me. My junior and senior years, I had my own room at the Campus Inn. I can't tell you why but someone set the room assignments and that's how it worked out. The wake up call was at 6:30 am sharp. I usually wore a half shirt that had a big blue football over the left breast. Above the football, was the word" Michigan" and below the ball it read "Football".

The shorts were the same grey cotton. I only wore them to get taped. You didn't want to offend any guests who might have wandered up to the "protected" area of the Inn.

Back at my room, I would dress as quickly as possible and head down to breakfast at 7:00 am sharp. Steak and eggs were always on the menu. It never varied.

At dinner, I used to put eight tabs of butter on the potato and then cover it with three to four tablespoons of sour cream. That was good stuff. No one ever told me it was unhealthy.

After breakfast there would be short position meetings. My position coach Tirrel Burton, never really had to remind Jim Smith, Rick White or myself of our game plan. After all, Smith was an All American and my game plan was, "run your man off or cut him at the knees." Coach Burton usually focused time on the younger guys. If we were playing a poor team, they'd be in that game in the second half anyway.

Some guys would go down and see their parents, or other family members in the lobby. I didn't think it was strange that my parents didn't come to many games. They just seemed so far away and they both had jobs that wouldn't be conducive to take every Friday off to fly 3000 miles to see their son play. I was by myself, but never really alone. I had all of my teammates with me!

Next was the thrill of the motorcade. Immediately out of the Campus Inn drive way the police escort lit up their lights and started the sirens. It was a short drive to the east end of the stadium, but it seemed to me that as we passed the tree lined streets in autumn you could feel Michigan Football in the air.

Most of the players adopted Bo's demeanor, serious, tough, and staring straight ahead. Obviously, there were some emotions that were caged and I never saw anyone get out of control prior to a game. There would be wooden barricades holding back the crowds that desperately wanted to get a look at the Wolverines.

After unloading the buses, we entered the locker room and that was where different rituals would emerge. What a time. What a great time.

CHAPTER 50
GAME TIME

This is the feeling just before the game. Can you feel it? It's the night before the fight. Things are beginning to get very, very clear. By that I mean something inside you clicks, and the world is much clearer, much more defined. I don't know what it is and I can't really explain it but your hearing is better, your eyes can see things they missed before and all your senses are on edge. I've asked myself 100 times, is this what a gladiator felt like just before he went out? Is this what was happening to the thousands of young men just before they hit the beach at Normandy? I won't ever have the answer, but I know it is a feeling that can't be described. The world is so clear and everything is moving so slowly, or am I moving faster?

There won't be much sleep tonight but that doesn't matter. There will be plenty of adrenaline in the tank by kick off. You can't recall eating dinner at the hotel but you know exactly what you had and how everything tasted so perfect….. but you ask yourself how did I eat?

There are jokes with your teammates and you laugh to ease the tremendous build up that is surging inside you. Is it nerves, is it tension, is it joy, is it the perfect state of bliss where mind and body function without thought or movement? It all happens so effortlessly. Bo comes by for bed check and asks if you are ready, even though he knows the answer. You lie awake in bed, and all that you hear is your heart pounding, reminding you that your body is ready, ready to give a supreme effort.

The next morning blows by, taping, breakfast, boarding the bus. The police escort blares its way to the Big House and a few thousand fans greet you at the entrance to the tunnel. As you dress, there is another transformation. Everything that was so clear over the last day now crystallizes into a whole new frame of mind. How could these colors be even more vibrant, features more defined? The world becomes surreal and yet at the same time you know your sole purpose in it. You buckle up and look up to see the wooden plaque, "Those Who Stay Will Be Champions". You reach up and slap the sign and begin the journey..........

CHAPTER 51
DUKE

On a Saturday, in mid September, my senior year, Duke University was coming into Ann Arbor to play us. It really wasn't supposed to be that good of a game. Somewhere, I had heard Duke hadn't won a game in four or five years. They were like the Northwestern of the ACC.

We had just trounced Illinois and had two tune ups (Duke and Navy) before we were to take on the powerful Texas A&M. They had a fullback bigger that anyone on our team and a kicker who was automatic from anywhere inside 60 yards (or so we heard).

The Duke game started off slowly and got slower as it progressed. I don't know what is was, but we were having trouble putting these Blue Devils away. Mind you, there was no question we were going to win the game. The question at hand was this, is Michigan going to win by a margin big enough to impress the rest of the football world?

We were driving for a score and we had just crossed mid field in the 3rd quarter. The play came in from the sidelines and Leach called "Red 38-39 check with me". This was a strong formation to the field (wide side). Red meant that the flanker and tight end both went to the right. I split out to the left or weak side. Mike Kenn was the weak-side tackle on my side. Once Leach got to the line he would look at the defense and determine which way we would run the play. The play was our standard option, either right (38), or left (39).

With this option play, Rick would put the ball in Russell Davis' belly and read where the defensive tackle was going. If the tackle came up field, Rick would let go and Russell would plow ahead with the ball. If the tackle crashed into Davis, Rick would pull the ball and run down to the defensive end and Russell would run through the tackle and, if he were good enough he would then try to run the safety over.

When Rick got to the end on the line, if the defensive end ran to the pitch Rick just turned up field with the ball himself. If the end came at Rick, he would pitch the ball to Huck around the end.

Since we had a tight end on the strong side, if we ran the play that way the tight end would leave the defensive end alone and seal the linebacker to the inside. If the play came my way, we didn't have the tight end on that side, so Mike Kenn would "pop" the defensive end and, then seal the linebacker on the backside.

Either way, the flanker (wide side) or split end (me on the short side) had to take on the defensive back, one on one. This might seem easy, as most defensive coaches would tell their defensive back's, "never let the receiver get deeper than you", and a well coached defensive back would just run off the ball with you and you could take him deep.

That only works when, and if, you ever throw the ball down the field, which we rarely did. The result was the defensive back's were usually flying up to the line the first time they read option.

This meant that your own personal war would take place somewhere between three to seven yards down field. In the 70's we were allowed to "cut" a player. I could throw myself at another player's knees and try to cut him down.

My strategy wasn't all that hard to figure out. If the defensive back was coming at me full tilt, thinking he was going to run through me I'd cut him. If he was cautious, I would stand and "chicken fight" (that's what Coach Hanlon used to call it). My first move would be to head butt him, if I could, and then, immediately try to whip my arms inside of his, so I could control his upper body with my hands. If the defensive back had the same technique, we often looked like two guys winging their arms up and down at each other on the film (hence "chicken fighting").

Back to the play. Rick gets to the line and barks out the signals, "Hit, Blue 39, Go" and off we went running the 39 option to my side. The defensive back ran off for the first seven to eight yards, then he read option, but he didn't fly up to the line. He squatted to make a play. I lowered myself to head butt him, however, he beat me to the whip and he actually knocked my left hand up, between both of our helmets, right when our heads met. BAM!

I swung my hips around and put my butt to the center of the field, trying to drive him out of bounds. The safety came up to make the tackle after about a 10-yard gain for Huck.

I ran back to the huddle, and when I bent over I could see that my ring finger on my left hand was bleeding. I wiped it on my pants, and noticed that the fingernail had been torn completely off. It was throbbing a little and bleeding. I looked around for the fingernail, but couldn't find it.

We lined up for the next play, and when I got into my stance, I saw that my fingernail was stuck to the shoulder pad of the Duke player I had blocked on the play earlier. Fortunately, the play was away to the other side and we both just kind of chased the play. When the play was over I reached up and plucked my nail off his shoulder pad and ran over to the sidelines.

I don't know what I was thinking, but I asked Lindsey McLean, our trainer, if he could put it back on (what can I say…I was 21, and that had never happened to me before). He said, "No, but we can use it as a pad." He stuck it back on and put tape over the whole mess. After the game, the whole thing came off and I had to deal with it in the training room.

The next Monday, when we went out to practice Lindsey told me he had a solution. He showed me half of one of those plastic things that kids get out of gum ball machines that could hold a toy ring or something. He wanted to fill that with gauze and then tape it around my finger.

I went out with the contraption and it looked like I had a mini light bulb on my ring finger. When I went in to hold for field goal practice, I couldn't catch the snap, so I tore the whole thing off and just went on without covering it. It healed in about two weeks.

What's funny about this is two weeks later, the Detroit Free Press came out their insert in the Sunday paper. The insert, was titled "Detroit" and the cover was a picture of Bo, with his telephone, giving me a play to run in, and if you look real hard you can see I don't have a fingernail on my ring finger of my left hand. My roommates and I had a good laugh over that one.

CHAPTER 52

BEFORE THE STORM

Everyone always asks, "What was it like in the locker room right before the game?" Well, a ton of things were going on. We usually got to the locker room a few hours before the game. The guys who had easy tape jobs got them done at the hotel before we left, so only the massive tape jobs on player's knees were left to pregame locker room. (Although they don't really tape knees anymore because there are wraps, sleeves, and braces that can handle the job better than tape.) Usually, guys were very serious from the time they got on the bus until they got inside the locker room. Then you would see a hundred different variations: sleeping, joking, pacing, fidgeting, resting, and so on. I bet the majority of guys today are plugged into iPods. We didn't even have cassette headphones back then, so you had to deal with anyone and everyone who wanted to talk to you.

It took me about five minutes to get out of my clothes and into the maize pants. I wore three pairs of socks: two on my feet that I pulled up as high as I could and one with the toes cut out that I pulled up to mid–thigh. I wore these to prevent "rug burns" from the tartan turf. Otherwise the carpet could rip your skin, and the small carpet fibers could get caught in the wound and infect the area. I tried to prevent carpet burns my entire career, but I was completely unsuccessful and lived the last three years at Michigan with oozing scabs on both elbows and occasionally a knee. I wore a jock without a cup, and I never wore the shorts underneath the pants. Part of our uniform was a wrap around girdle that had foam butt pads and two hip protectors. I cut the butt pad in half and purposely wore the hip protectors so they stuck up outside my pants. Then I tucked sweet number eighty-five inside all of this and proceeded to the shoes. I wore the Adidas Allstars, and I tied them as tight as I possibly could. I also had the tightest tape jobs on the team. I didn't feel right unless my toes turned a little purple and my legs felt like casts from my mid calf through my ankle. I wasn't about to break an ankle on that carpet-covered concrete. Then I'd slip on elbow sleeves, and I was ready for warm-ups.

During my first year on the field, I tried to take in everything around me at the same time. This made it hard to concentrate. My sophomore year, I was totally sucked into what happened on the field. By my junior and senior years, the game and pregame felt like they slowed way down. I had time to look into the stands and joke around a little. Remember the player that caught the ball behind his back on the long ball warm-ups? I started that little trick.

Once we went back into the locker room to get our shoulder pads on, the tenor usually changed. Emotion started to build, and players began their funny, superstitious routines such as high fiving all the starters. I usually read the program to see if I knew anyone on the other team. Some of the guys had to use the can because of nervous energy, and some had to use the same stall every time, every game. Imagine a line of five guys waiting to use a stall—the same stall—even though there were three other stalls open. I'll tell you, some superstitions are really strange. That said, we all felt the same way: whatever a guy needed to do to make sure he felt "right" and ready to play, let him do it.

In the last few minute before the game, it was unusually quiet. Then an official would pop his head in the door and holler, "Two minutes, two minutes." Bo would approach the blackboard and give one of his patented pep talks. They could take you from a state of keen readiness to one of euphoria in about thirty seconds. You would gladly run head first into a brick wall if he asked you. Then there was a controlled riot to touch the plaque above the door and flow out into the tunnel.

Was there a heaven? Was there a hell? There surely was on Saturdays in the fall in Ann Arbor: Heaven was wearing that beautiful winged helmet. As for that other place … you'd have to ask the guys who played against Michigan in the seventies.

CHAPTER 53

TEXAS A&M

The Michigan-Texas A&M game was supposed to be an epic battle: the first big game of the 1977 season. Texas A&M had the nation's most feared wishbone attack, with Mark Mosley as quarterback and Curtis Dickey as one of the running backs. If that wasn't enough, we also had to deal with unstoppable George Woodard, the nation's most feared fullback, weighing in at over 280 pounds. Even if we were lucky enough to stop this unbeatable rushing attack, the Aggies were assured three points as their kicker, Tony Franklin, could hit a field goal from seventy yards out. We were ranked either two or three depending on the poll, and so was Texas A&M.

When the game started, the tartan field was damp and wet. Bo had personally challenged our defense to make sure they knew that this would be their toughest test. The defensive line of Curt Greer, Chris Godfrey, and Dale "Chunky" Keitz had to play their best game. The ends, Dominic Tedesco and John Anderson, had to play both the quarterback and pitch in the Bone option attack. The linebackers perhaps faced the toughest test. They had to make sure big Woodard didn't get the ball. If he did, oh brother, they had to bring him down. This would have been a chore for Ron Simpkins as he only weighed 230 pounds, a full 45 to 50 pounds less than "Woo Woo" Woodard. For Jerry Meter, who weighed 205 pounds, it was unthinkable. If Woo Woo didn't have the ball, the linebackers had to sprint to stop the quarterback from turning upfield.

If all of that didn't happen, they had to chase down the running back to get the pitch. Curtis Dickey, we were told, ran the hundred-yard dash in 9.3 seconds, faster than anyone on our defense. This was going to be our toughest challenge.

A&M also had the fastest linebackers and toughest tackles in the Big Twelve. They practiced against the option offense all the time as that was all they saw when they played Oklahoma, Nebraska, and Texas. Neither team was going to fool the other with trick plays. Instead, we'd have to look the other guys in the eye and say, "Buckle up baby, and show me what you've got." This was smash-mouth football at its best.

The first series ended with Franklin kicking a field goal. We all thought, "Damn, we can't let them cross midfield again." The slugfest continued, and Michigan held a slim 7–3 advantage going into halftime.

In the locker room at halftime, it was encouraging to hear Simpkins and Greer tell the entire team that Texas A&M would not score again. Our offense boasted, "We have a fullback and his name is Russell Davis and he's going to outrush Woo Woo." On the first drive of the second half, our big line punished the Aggie defense, and Russell ripped off huge gains. Eventually he punched one into the end zone. I knelt for the extra point and promptly let the snap slip through my fingers. It was wet, but I should have made the play. I picked up the fumble and was immediately swarmed over by Aggies.

We were still up 13–3. We forced a quick punt, and Dwight Hicks fielded the punt right at midfield. After a few plays, we had the ball down near their thirty-five yard line. Bo sent in the play: "White tight eighty-one cross-country with motion." We had run eighty-one cross-country for the last two years: the tight end and the wingback crossed over the middle, goofing up the linebackers. Then Leach would pick whom he wanted to throw the ball to. But in this version, "white tight," we would have two tight ends and no wingback. This week we had added another element, "motion," which meant that I would motion back toward the tight end on my side, and at the snap, I would split the middle of the field. We hoped that I would draw both the wide-side cornerback and the safety away from the wide side of the field. At the same time, the tight ends would cross. We hoped that the linebackers would cover one or both of the tight ends. If they covered only one, then Leach would have an easy throw for a ten-yard gain. If they covered both, then we were off to the races. Why did this play work so well? It worked because we were also running a "wheel"—where the back runs to the wide side of the field and jets right up the sideline—with Roosevelt Smith. There was no way a linebacker could stay with Rosy.

We thought we had all our options covered; here's what happened: Leach raised his heel, my signal to go in motion. When I was about five yards from our tight end, Gene Johnson, Leach barked out "Go!" and the line went into pass protection. The tight ends crossed, both covered by linebackers. Leach dropped back looks at Rosy and saw that the safety had jumped him in "man-to-man" coverage. Rick immediately knew that I also had to be covered man to man by the cornerback, and I had a running start because I was in motion. With no safety in the middle of the field, I was wide open. So Rick fired the ball deep to me! I had run by everyone, so I actually had to slow down to judge the flight of the ball. Since I had dropped the snap earlier, my concentration was on high alert. I cradled the ball in just as the cornerback reached up and grabbed my facemask. He pulled hard and my head twisted, but there was no way I was going to drop that pass. The stadium erupted, and I was mobbed by the team. Touchdown Michigan!

Wally and Big Fella lifted me over their shoulders. As I knelt for the extra point, the Big House was rocking. One hundred five thousand fans chanted in unison, "We're number one; we're number one," and the sound was deafening.

The floodgates had opened. Simpkins blocked a punt that Pickens recovered for a touchdown. Mike Jolly intercepted a pass and returned it for a touchdown. Anyone who went out for a hot dog when the score was 13–3, came back to a 41–3 score. It was over! We had our third team in midway through the fourth quarter. As I watched from the sidelines, two things struck me: First, our defense was awesome and true to their word that Texas A&M would not score again. Second, our fullback had rushed for an average of 5.75 yards per carry and scored two touchdowns. Woo Woo averaged 3.8 yards and did not score after some forty carries. As I stood on the fifty looking across the field, I yelled at the top of my lungs, "We have a fullback too!"

The ref never called the facemask grab against me, but it didn't matter. I didn't even know about it until we reviewed the film, although my neck was sore the day after the game. Everything happened so fast.

I did take some heat from some of my buddies, though. The catch was the headline for both the Ann Arbor News and the Detroit Free Press. It was also featured in an article that Sports Illustrated did on the "Big Game" that week. Michigan vaulted to number one in both polls afterward. We were right back where we belonged … again.

Texas A&M's, Jim Hamilton grabbing Curt Stephenson's face mask in the 3rd quarter

Forget the facemask. The team celebrates Stephenson's touchdown
against Texas A&M

CHAPTER 54

MSU, 1977

The 1977 Michigan-MSU game was unique in the annals of Wolverine rivalries. When I first got into football there were only a few teams that caught my attention: the mid–sixties Notre Dame and MSU games were a thrill, so was the UCLA and MSU Rose Bowl game. The Clinton Jones, George Webster, and Bubba Smith teams impressed me. In the late sixties, the Buckeyes, led by Rex Kern and Jim Otis, seemed invincible, but as you know, they were not. So I fell for the Maize and Blue. There was something about Bo, the colors, and that winged helmet that was just irresistible.

When I got to Michigan I learned the story of the Little Brown Jug and the rivalry with Minnesota. There was a ferocious rivalry between Michigan and Ohio State. There was a coastal rivalry between USC and Michigan. But nothing could compare to the rivalry between Michigan and Michigan State.

I knew when I got to school that we had a rivalry with Michigan State, but it seemed so … one sided. We took MSU seriously every year even though most of the games were lopsided: 31–0 and 21–7 in our favor. We had spanked them 42–10 the year before. It seemed that the rivalry meant more to MSU than it did to Michigan. They hated and detested the Wolverines. Coming from California, I wasn't aware of this until I experienced it firsthand. Even then it didn't make much sense. For the rivalry to have meaning for me, I needed the games to matter, like if they determined the Big Ten Champ or the Rose Bowl representative. In my years at Michigan, the game was just another Big Ten game on our way to the Championship. If Michigan State had ever beaten us, it would have made their year. But they still would never have gone to the Rose Bowl. Whereas if we lost, we still had a shot at the Rose Bowl if we went on to beat Ohio State. It just seemed that they hyped up the game more than we did.

Well, in 1977, they had a pretty good team led by a good-sized, speedy wideout named Kirk Gibson. Ed Smith was their quarterback. We played the game in East Lansing, which was never an easy place to play. On Friday we worked out in the Big House and then traveled to Jackson, Michigan to spend the night. Early the next morning we ate breakfast at the hotel and re-boarded the buses for East Lansing. This meant we arrived on the day of the game rather than going a day ahead of time to work out in the MSU stadium.

Arriving at a stadium was always interesting on the road. Onlookers quietly sized us up, and the stadium was eerily silent. The only two places in the Big Ten where we heard fans were MSU and OSU. Their shouts were always the same: cat calls, something personal about one of our mothers, or, more often, a stream of profanity (like we were supposed to be offended). They were never very creative.

The visitor's lockers also were not particularly imaginative. Hayden Fry at Iowa painted the visitors' lockers pink. I thought that was sort of funny. At MSU, the lockers were concrete gray with a two-by-six board bolted into the wall about five feet high. Metal hooks (one per player) jutted out from the two-by-six for our clothes. Again, this didn't matter. We were accustomed to this belittling treatment, and it wasn't going to sway us from our goal to win the championship.

The game started slowly; neither team gained an advantage. After a Leach fumble in our own territory, MSU capitalized quickly when Ed Smith hit Gibson for a nineteen yard touchdown. That pissed off our defense. On the next kickoff, we marched eighty yards for the tying score. Right before the half we got the ball back and mustered a few first downs, but we got bogged down and faced a fourth down on the MSU forty yard line. Bo called out, "field goal" and out trotted Greg "Peeps" Wilner. Greg was about 5'8" and all of 145pounds. He had never attempted a fifty yarder in a game before, let alone on the road. Peeps also happened to be Michigan's first, soccer style kicker. The previous four years we had Mike Lantry and Bobby Wood who were both straight on toe kickers. I knelt at the MSU forty, took the snap, spun the laces in front, put the ball down, and tilted it just the way Peeps liked it. The second he hit it, I knew it was good. I could tell by how solid the contact was and how it sounded. I never saw the ball go through the uprights. I just stood up and gave Peeps a big hug. We went into half time up 10–7.

In the second half, MSU couldn't hold on to the ball. I think this was a result of our defense rather than the rain that had begun to fall. James Early fumbled on our twenty-six yard line, and we marched the other seventy-four yards for a score a new score of 17–7. Dwight Hicks then intercepted a pass and took it back to the MSU six yard line. Leach ran the option to perfection and scored two plays later for a 24–7 lead. Hicks had also knocked Kirk Gibson out of the game with a terrific hit.

MSU managed to score with eight minutes left when Ed Smith hit Early with an eleven yard scoring pass. But all we had to do was field the kickoff and run out the clock. MSU kicked off and we pounded out a couple of first downs. However, MSU was tough and stopped us around our thirty-five yard line. As I mentioned before, Bo had put me on the punt team. For whatever reason MSU didn't block me, and I released free on our punt. The entire fourth quarter was played in a downpour, and our punter, John Anderson, didn't get off a very good punt. It swirled in the wind, and as I ran under it for coverage it took a weird bounce and hit a Spartan blocker in the leg. I immediately jumped on the ball at the MSU forty yard line and we ran out the clock for our fifth win in a row. Both the UPI and AP wire services voted Michigan number one in the polls. The following week when we hosted Wisconsin who was also undefeated, there was talk of that becoming a rivalry game. Yeah, right. We kicked their fannies too, 56–0.

Stephenson congratulates Greg Wilner on his 50 yard field goal against
MSU

CHAPTER 55

BO BEFORE OSU

This chapter takes us back to November 19, 1977. Pre–game was over. I was fully dressed, had a good sweat going, and was totally at ease with myself. I was about to play my last game in the Big House, Michigan Stadium. I tried to make it last as long as possible, but everything was flying by.

The championship was on the line. (What else was new?) There were one hundred ten thousand fans in the stands, the vast majority cheering for us to beat Ohio State so that we could again represent the Big Ten in the Rose Bowl. As I sat on my stool in front of my locker, my feet tapped nervously. I looked up and Bo had moved to the center of the room.

"Gentlemen, we now move to the last step of a journey that started a year ago when we walked off the field as champions in Columbus," he said.

"We set our goals for 1977. They were lofty. We agreed to commit to work as hard as we could to win the Big Ten title and go to the Rose Bowl. When we started, I told you that those who stayed would be champions. Along that journey some left us for whatever reasons, but those of you who stayed are part of something special. You stayed because you care about Michigan Football. You care about your school, your teammates, and you care about yourselves. You are now going to be part of the greatest rivalry game in college football. This is special. There are only a handful of people that will get to play in this game, and here you are.

142

The question at hand is how will you perform? How do you want to be remembered? Your moment is now. This is not about tomorrow. It is not about yesterday. It is about what you will do in the next three hours. Look around the room; look at the guy next to you. How do you want him to remember you? How do you want him to remember how you played in the greatest college football game? Thirty years from now when we have our team reunion you'll all see each other again. Wouldn't it be great to shake each other's hands and see a championship ring? What glorious memories that will bring back.

"We have prepared for this game for twelve months. The running, the sweating, the hard practices have all led to this point. The time is now. When you take the field remember this:

"One: Play with passion. For you seniors, this is the last game you will play in Michigan Stadium. Remember all the great past players who have been in this same position. Play for their memory. They will be in the stands cheering Michigan on. For you underclassmen, play with passion; do not take this game for granted. You have earned the right to play here but this situation may never present itself again. Play this game like you will never play again. Play it as though every play is the last play that you will ever make. Make it you best play.

"Two: Play with poise. You are Michigan. There will be mistakes out there. Once over, they are forgotten. A Michigan man always plays with poise. Trust that the man next to you will have your back, and we will win as a team.

"Three: Play with pride. You are wearing the greatest uniform and helmet in all of college football. No team, no university has ever won more than Michigan. You came to this great university to be in the exact position you are in right now. Relish it. Absorb it.

"OK, men, we're ready. Ready to add to the great history of Michigan Football. Ready to be *champions*! Let's go."

With that Bo smacked the blackboard and knocked it over. The room erupted, and we poured into the tunnel and onto the field. The roar of the fans was almost deafening.

The memory is so clear; I see it like it was yesterday. Damn, I love Michigan Football.

CHAPTER 56

WOODY AND ME

A lot has been written about the "Ten Year War" between OSU and Michigan—Bo and Woody—from 1969 until 1978. I was there for the fun from 1973 until November 1977. These games were some of the greatest moments in Michigan history. They played a big part in the structure of the conference and how people across the country view football today.

The Michigan-OSU rivalry was the biggest that there was in sports. Some people might argue with that statement, but they are simply wrong. There was nothing bigger than Ohio State and Michigan, and there was no bigger part of that rivalry than Bo and Woody. I was blessed to be a part of that. In 1977, I was firmly entrenched in the lore that surrounded the game.

Woody was known for his temper. Many people witnessed it when he tore up the yard markers after Tom Darden intercepted a pass in the 1971 game. I wasn't ever recruited by the man but heard countless stories about him from guys like Rob Lytle, Dennis Franklin, Dave Brown, and scores of other Midwestern players. He loved you as long as you were interested in OSU, but if you took another side, he wouldn't talk to you until after you graduated. I didn't realize it until years later, as I was watching an old tape of the 1977 Michigan-OSU game, he punched a cameraman late in the game and it was caught on national TV.

I have my own personal Woody story. The 1977 game, like all the others, determined who would be the Rose Bowl representative for the Big Ten. The championship was on the line again. OSU had a great team, led by Rod Gerald at quarterback. He was shifty and quick. Ron Springs was the tailback. And they had a great defense led by Tom Cousineau. We weren't too bad either, with an offense that had the best line in the nation with Leach, Russell Davis, and Huckleby in the backfield. Our defense was equally as tough with John Anderson, Ron Simpkins, Curt Greer, Dwight Hicks, and Mel Owens. It was going to be one of those good old fashion smash mouth games. These usually weren't fun to watch and often offered everyone involved a chance to down large quantities of antacid and aspirin.

It was a cool and damp day. I got on the bus from the Campus Inn and looked at the trees as the police escort blared its way to the stadium. All of the leaves had fallen from the trees, a sure sign that winter was about to settle in. When we arrived at the Big House, throngs of fans cheering for us to win another championship greeted us. Most of us dressed in silence like we usually did as this was serious business we had to attend to. The team went out early for stretching and pre–game, and OSU was nowhere to be seen. After twenty-five minutes or so, Bo told the troops it was time to go up.

Coach Jerry Hanlon was both the offensive line coach and the special teams coach. He asked that Greg "Peeps" Wilner, our kicker; George Lilja, our snapper; and yours truly, the holder, stay out and take a few extra as it was damp outside. So we lined up and hit a few extra kicks. Coach Hanlon then told us to get up to the locker room, and we ran toward the tunnel. Ohio State entered the tunnel from their locker room at the same time. Ohio State ran down the tunnel about ninety strong. They were four to five players wide and took up most of the tunnel at the entrance to the field. Hanlon ran up the opposite side of the tunnel. and we followed him in single file. George Lilja was first, followed by Greg Wilner, and then me. I was behind the others I wanted to cherish every second on the field during my last game at Michigan.

No one really talked to each other in the tunnel, but you could hear some of the Buckeyes egging each other on with "Kick their ass" and the age old favorite "F— Michigan." One voice was louder than all the others; it was Woody. He was the last to leave the locker room, and I didn't see him until we were half way up. He was hollering at the top of his lungs trying to fire his guys up. His team was basically out on the field and it was curious that Woody started to drift over to us hollering the whole way. He ran right past Lilja (George was 6'5" and maybe 270 pounds), and when he passed Wilner, Peeps turned and faced the tunnel wall. I looked up just in time to see Woody's fist coming right at my head. Mind you I was wearing a helmet and shoulder pads so he could not hurt me. Instincts took over, and I dodged the blow. His fist missed, but his forearm hit my shoulder pad flush. My first thought was how surreal this whole scene was. This was the biggest game of the biggest rivalry in the entire country, and I was squared off against perhaps the most famous coach in the nation. The Ohio State team stopped at the base of the tunnel, and Hanlon grabbed Wilner and pushed him into our locker room. For what seemed like an eternity Woody and I stared at each other. I think he was waiting for me to do something … and I did. I started to laugh at the absurdity of the whole situation. Woody turned to the field and ran out of the tunnel. Coach Hanlon came over to me and asked what had happened as he hadn't seen the blow. I told him "nothing." I didn't want anything to detract from the game.

You all know that Huck couldn't play so we started Roosevelt Smith at tailback. Both he and Leach found pay dirt, and we logged fourteen points. Simpkins and Greer played a whale of a game, and OSU never got close to our end zone. All they could muster was a few field goals. The 1976 win in Columbus was one of the most satisfying experiences of my life. It was an outpouring of all the build up from past OSU matches that we should have won. The joy was prolonged because we knew from our first touchdown on we weren't going to lose. The 1977 game was more of an instant rush. When Gerald fumbled and Derek Howard fell on the ball with a few minutes to go, we knew we had it won. We were going to the Rose Bowl again! The great thing about this game was that it was in front of 106,000 deserving Michigan fans.

As we were running out the clock, I split way out—all the way to the Ohio State sideline. I made sure Woody's eyes met mine. I said, "Hey, fatman, what do you think now?" It wasn't original, and it was probably uncalled for. There are times when I regret saying it. But I said it in the heat of battle, and I can't take it back. I've forgiven Woody for what happened; he, too, was in the heat of battle. Afterward, Jon Falk and a few of the coaches told me not to talk about it to the press. They said Woody was an icon. He was at the end of his career, and it wouldn't do anyone any good. Woody ended that career eleven months later when he hit that Clemson kid on national TV. Today, my story is just another good tale to add to the Michigan versus Ohio State ongoing war.

CHAPTER 57

A MICHIGAN MAN

A lot of talk, opinions, and assumptions have gone into defining the "Michigan Man." Being called a Michigan Man by someone who is a Michigan Man is a great honor. As, some of you may know, the root of the phrase lies with Bo who also coined the phrase, "Those who stay will be champions." Both phrases can mean a variety of things and can be quite different depending on someone's view. It may sound bizarre, but the phrase, "Those who stay" means something different to Michigan fans than it meant for the players who Bo originally spoke those words. The phrase grew over time and gained new meanings.

The same can be said for the phrase "Michigan Man." By its strict definition you cannot be a Michigan Man unless you were directly involved in the football program and you possessed certain qualities that elevated you to Michigan Man status. To be a Michigan Man a person had to commit himself to Michigan, to the program, and to living clean. He had to support the essence of the Michigan program by Bo's standards. If a person was a true believer in Michigan football—even if they were not a part of the blood, sweat, and tears of the physical program—they could become one with the program and become a Michigan Man. This would take total commitment, nothing less. A person would need to fully dedicate himself to winning the right way to reach the mountain top Only then could he find total nirvana, total completion. It is not easy, and it has yet to be fulfilled at Michigan. There are teams that have come close and fans that have come close. It is what we strive for every year.

Can Rich Rodriguez get us there? Yes, he can. He may do it in another way, but he has the tools in front of him. He may need to spend some time with the "old guard" to understand the concept of a Michigan Man. It isn't simply talking about the concept, but living it day to day in life. Dan Dierdorf could verbalize this concept and so could Jamie Morris. I hope I've done a little bit to help people understand it.

A Michigan Man is totally committed to the program. He is in the program either in body and spirit (as a player) or in spirit only if he cannot be in body (like Bo when he was a little boy dreaming of great Michigan Football or Lloyd Carr when he accepted the job to be a coach at Michigan before he even landed on campus). Either way he is totally committed. A Michigan Man thinks first and foremost about what will make the program the standard others strive to achieve. This means winning within the rules, being the best in football and in academics, and having respect for others even if they scorn him. He does what he knows is right not what others tell him to and not necessarily what is easiest. It means even if his son plays for USC, he knows and understands that he *has* to sit on the Michigan side at the Rose Bowl, even when the rest of his loving family sits on the USC side. The pressure can be great, but he must stay the course. This is the only way to live as a Michigan Man. If the current and future Michigan coaches get this commitment, then I have comfort that Michigan can be the envy of the football world for another thirty-five years. Wouldn't that be something?

CHAPTER 58
BO, ONE-ON-ONE

Bo coached for twenty years. With approximately thirty-five new players per year, dozens of coaches, hundreds of sports writers, professors, other team's coaches, he touched a lot of people's lives and they all have a Bo story. There are literally thousands of stories that revolve around Bo.

The media image of the sour-puss, ranting, raving, and determined coach was only true to a very small degree. There were some players who absolutely feared the man. I should know; I was one of them until the start of my junior year. After all, he controlled whether I got onto the field to play, which meant more to me than anything my first few years. I started with a dream, and he gave me a shot. After that, my goals were small: I wanted to make the travel squad, then I wanted a lot of play time, and finally I wanted to start. Once these were realized, a whole new set of goals came into to play. My fear of Bo retreated and he became my "second dad." I know that every player has a different relationship with Bo, and I can't compare myself to anyone else. I felt he had a certain place in his heart for a guy like me. I was a Donnie Warner kind of guy who came from nowhere, with no hype, and persevered. Bo loved that stuff. He wouldn't show it on the field or in the meeting rooms. I don't know if he ever told "old Stephenson" stories to players after I left the program. I do know we had something special, and I will cherish my time with him until I pass.

No one really got much one-on-one with Bo unless he was the starting quarterback. However, at the end of each school year each and every scholarship player met one-on-one with Bo. I didn't have one in 1974 as I wasn't on scholarship. In 1975 my meeting with him was all of two minutes because I told him I was going home to La Jolla for the summer. He was not happy with that and cut off the meeting. In 1976, the meeting was rather formal as he was expecting me to start at receiver. But it just covered the basics like grades, roommates, and summer job status. During the 1976 season a lot happened. For one, I was his starting split end on a team that had won the Big Ten Championship and had gone on to play USC in the Rose Bowl. During the year, my roommate had lost his scholarship due to a variety of poor decisions. My other roommate had been injured for two seasons and was generally considered crazy by everyone's ledger. So when I entered his office for my one-on-one, I knew we would be spending a fair amount of time covering these issues.

Right out of the chute Bo said, "I can't afford you and Kenn to get mixed up with those guys (our two roommates). You know what I mean?"

"Yes, sir," I said.

He looked at some papers in front of him and blurted out, "Looks like you got a 4.0 last semester. How many semesters in a row at 4.0?"

"Just two, sir," I responded.

He retorted, "I'd figure a smart kid like you would know what not to do, right?"

"Yes, sir", was my response.

"OK, I got you for one more year. Can I count on you to give me your best?"

Again, I responded, "Yes, sir."

Then he floored me. "My sources tell me you're seeing a tall blond over at the Theta house and you have been for the last year. Is there anything there?"

How did he know *that*? All I could muster was, "Excuse me?"

He asked if she was a good Midwestern girl and where her parents were from. The conversation turned more into a father asking his son about his intentions. He wanted to know where I was going to live next year because he had heard that Mike Kenn and I would not be roommates. He was relived when I told him I was moving to McKinley, right across the street from Yost.

"Correct, sir."

I told him that I was going to live in Ann Arbor again that summer and planned to work at the GM proving grounds. Again, he told me that some of his players either got married going into their senior year or right after school, and he wanted to know if there was anything he could do to help. He wanted me to know that if I ended up with a quality girl from the Midwest than I was as smart a kid as he thought I was. He told me he wished more of his meetings went like ours because it did him good to know that there were guys he could count on. It was the first time he and I had a conversation where he showed a good deal of concern for where I was and where I was going. For me it was a break through; that's when he became more than just my coach. He didn't extend himself like he had done for some other players, but he showed me he cared, and our relationship grew over the next year. I sort of took his advice: although I didn't marry the Theta, I did marry another tall, blond, Midwestern gal, and I have been happy with that choice for more than twenty-eight years. Bo was like a second father to me, and I can't thank him enough. I was just some kid 2500 miles from home, and the only really mentor I had was probably the most powerful guy in the State of Michigan. I say that with respect to the Governor and the Senators of the State of Michigan. I say that with confidence because they knew deep down they would have had to quit if Bo had ever run for office. Right? You know I'm right. They all are lucky that Bo only wanted one thing in life, and that was to be a football coach. I couldn't have asked for a better mentor, teacher, coach, or friend. Those days at Michigan were some of the best of my life.

CHAPTER 59

LOSING BO

When Bo passed away, we all lost something special. You lost an icon. I lost a coach, a mentor, a teacher, and a second father. Dan Dierdorf said, "There aren't many the likes of Bo that walk the face of this earth." He was right: there aren't many. There should be more. I said, " I wish this country had ten thousand Bo Schembechlers." I still believe that today. We would be much better off if that were true. Our vision of ourselves would be clearer, our purpose brighter, our goals right in front of us so we could grab and cherish them.

It is so hard to put into words what Bo meant to me. There were a thousand guys who played for him and coached with him who know exactly what I mean. But we can't seem to say it because it comes at us on so many different levels. Coach, teacher, mentor, advisor, leader, way of life. He was filled with honesty, integrity, emotions, strength, motivation, clarity. I could go on and on.

He's famous for saying "I don't care if you black, white, or green I'll treat you all the same ... I'll treat you like dogs." He'd say that with a sparkle in his eye and that little turned up smile that would say, "You don't know if I'm kidding or if I'm really like this do you?" You know what? He may have treated us like dogs, but he loved every dog he ever coached, and he would stand up for that dog through thick or thin. We were his "boys," and he loved to see us shine well past the football field, well into life.

In 1985, when he brought out the Harbaugh led Wolverines to play Nebraska in the Fiesta Bowl they had a huge luncheon at some resort in Scottsdale. I flew from San Diego to visit a few days before the game. I didn't call him or tell anyone I was coming in. As soon as I landed, I drove my rental car to the resort, and I made it just as they were serving lunch. There were a hundred people at the long head table in front of three thousand guests. All were waiting to hear Bo and Tom Osborne speak about the game. I snuck around the back of the room and climbed up the dais.

I walked behind Bo, got him in a chokehold, and said, "Guess who?"

He growled, "If you're a skinny runt from La Jolla, all I have to say is that there's only been one guy who ever came outta there that was worth his salt, and it took me a few years to get him there."

I let go, he stood up, and we hugged each other. He turned to the head table and announced he was going to be late with his speech because he had to catch up with me. I told him there was no way I was going to interrupt him; I had only swung by to say hi. In vintage Bo he said, "Finding out what you're up to is going to be way more fun and important than this damn lunch". So we spent thirty minutes talking while all the other dignitaries were introduced and gave their speeches. That was classic Bo.

The man was as much an influence on me as my parents, and in a beautiful way, I hope I have passed on some of his traits through my teachings to my kids. I'd rather create ten thousand new Bo's than write down my memories of him. We can encourage more people to be like him, you know, it isn't that hard. All we have to do is be honest, posses the utmost integrity and character, have a passion for life, and share that with everyone. Talk about vision. Talk about a gift for future generations. Imagine a world like that. I'm going to try and do my part to help his legacy live on forever. Come on; join the Wolverine team that he's built. You never know who or what or when you can influence someone!

CHAPTER 60

COACHING AND WINNING

Winning *a* football game isn't really all that hard to do. All you have to do is outscore your opponent. Winning football games consistently is much harder. And winning championships is even harder than that. When you say that you will win, win consistently, win championships, and do it all by a certain code and within the rules then it becomes damn near impossible. Especially when the code committed you to play the game fairly, with honor, with respect for your opponent, and with class— that separated your effort from all of the others and best represented your school.

You can win with talent. You can win with character. When you have a combination of both, you have a shot at greatness. To sustain this combination of talent and character for decades, you have to have a leader who is willing to sacrifice his life and soul to the proposition that there is a certain way to conduct yourself. There is a certain way to practice, a certain way to prepare.

Once you have this there are two more ingredients that make up the winning formula. The first is hard work. You need commitment at every level to work harder than anyone else. The coaching staff, the players, the trainers, the medical staff, the strength and conditioning personnel, the administration, the tutors, the recruiters, and on and on must all be committed. The second and probably most important thing that you need is passion. If every single person doesn't have intense passion then your program is at risk. Passion comes from within. It is born of the marriage of love and commitment. It thrives in an environment of pride, accomplishment, and desire. What the mind can conceive (desire and commitment), and mind can achieve (accomplishment) and those who stay will be champions. It is true, simple, and accurate.

The man who taught me these lessons was Bo. Only he didn't have to sacrifice his soul to accomplish this. That was just the way Bo lived his life, which should give you a glimpse of what made him so unique. Hard work, that was just his make up. Desire, part of his genes. Commitment, there wasn't a soul on this earth more committed than Bo. Passion, all you had to do was watch him on the sidelines. Love, just ask any of his players.

Now, when that coach has all of those ingredients, he then needs to mold his players. Football is a rough nasty game, and you need rough nasty guys to play the game. But they also must have the ability to turn this nastiness on and off. It must be on when they are on the field and off when they are doing anything other than football. That is the real character building exercise.

For some players it is easier to act tough than it is for others. There are two kinds of toughness: mental and physical. Mental toughness is ten times more important in football than physical toughness. I state this for two main reasons: First, physical toughness comes from being mentally tough. Most people don't like to hit other people. Second, everyone at the D-1 level works out and has the ability to improve their strength and stamina. Strength coaches create specific programs to make guys physically stronger and tougher. Therefore, each player can achieve his best physical strength. What holds players back is the mental side. If they believe they can lift more weight or run faster, then they will break through the previous barriers that held them back. The result will be more confidence and more achievement because achievement is a mental process, not a physical one. As someone gets stronger, they can dominate on the field by through strength or quickness.

On the other hand, there is not a set program to make someone mentally tougher. There are no specific exercises like squats or bench press. There are masters, however, at the mental toughing game. Bo was one of these masters. This is where a coach can effect a huge change in his players.

At a base level, most people don't like to hit other people the way they have to in football. Over time certain people learn to hit, realize that they can do this, and start to enforce their will on others. It is at this point that a player will begin "liking" to hit others. Some learn this in high school. Others learn this in college. What a truly great coach does is take that type of individual and teach him to do this over and over, consistently. Once this is achieved, the coach needs to expand the player's mental toughness. This includes building confidence that allows the athlete to react automatically in pressure situations. Every coach knows that a player starts to question his abilities when he is tired or when he's been beaten a few times in a row. It is all mental.

Bo was a genius at maximizing player's mental stamina. He knew that by pushing us both physically and mentally, we would be better players. Our practices were harder than the games. As a receiver, for example, if you survived going over the middle when Dave Brown or Don Dufek hit you right in the chops, then you knew you could go back over the middle again. Was it fun? Hell no, it wasn't suppose to be. But if I had to go over the middle against Purdue, it was a walk in the park compared to practice.

People ask, "Did Bo yell at you in practice?" You have to be kidding me! It isn't patty cake out there. It is football, and all these guys love to hit. To be competitive you have to make sure all the aspects are covered. Sure he hollered. He yelled to his heart's content, but we knew that he had a reason for it. It was for our own good. If you made it through you knew that the guy next to you was just as tough as you and then … then, my friend, you had team confidence. You had a close knit family willing to fight. You had a family willing to leave it all on the field and the confidence that the other team didn't come close to possessing that mental toughness.

Don't forget the first half of Bo's infamous quote, "What the mind can conceive and believe, the mind can achieve … and those who stay will be champions."

CHAPTER 61
ROSE BOWL EVENTS

Back in the late seventies, when Michigan went to the Rose Bowl, the team did some pretty cool things. Yes, we had double sessions, and we hit in both practices. That was just how Bo prepared his team. So the practices were rough, but our free time was not. Actually there wasn't much truly free time. When we weren't practicing, watching films, or in meetings, the coaching staff had us booked. Even though Bo hated for us to do these extra events, he was obligated because of the Rose Bowl contract. And they were fun for us! Our scheduled events included Disneyland, the "Beef" Bowl at Lawry's Prime Rib, *The Tonight Show, Starring Johnny Carson*, the Rose Bowl Float tour, and Universal Studios. Disneyland was always fun, even for a guy like me from California who had been there a hundred times. They closed off portions of the park as "Team Only" areas, and it was cool. My junior year was a little different because we were at the park at the same time as the USC team. The attendants let the players go to the front of the lines in the areas that were open to everyone, and the Rose Bowl Queen and her court followed us around. Most of these gals were seniors from local high schools. Plus all the television crews constantly followed us around. This was back when no one had hand held phones with videos cameras so if the TV crew wasn't there to witness shenanigans, they were never caught on tape.

We also attended *The Tonight Show, Starring Johnny Carson* at the same time as the USC team. Just before the show we filled out a card that had basic information about ourselves and questions that we wanted to ask Mr. Carson. Johnny Carson was probably the most famous TV host in the country at that time. Jay Leno and David Letterman patterned their shows after him. Both teams were seated way up in the nosebleed section, far away from the stage. I don't know if that was for economic reasons or out of fear that something might happen on live TV if we were too close to the action. I sat on the end of a row, and right across the aisle was a USC player, the big All-American tackle, Marvin Powell. Mr. Carson did his monologue and mentioned that he had the two mighty Rose Bowl teams in the audience. When he sat down with Ed McMahon, Johnny began to read through the cards that we had filled out. He pulled out a card from Marvin Powell and answered the question that Marvin had asked Johnny. Then I was shocked when Johnny started to read my card. He said something to the effect of, "Looks like Michigan has a receiver from La Jolla, California. Now wait a minute; why would anyone from La Jolla want to go to the winter wonderland?" The joke got some laughs, and he immediately went to another card. I wish I could have answered him. I would have loved to tell him about my dream, about Bo, and about the great experience I was having at U of M. However, he got a few laughs, and I got kidded by most of the Michigan team. Stuff like, "Surf, he doesn't know how dumb you really are. Not only did you go from paradise to the frozen tundra, you did it on a team that doesn't throw the ball. You're dumber than dumb!"

When we went to Lawry's, Bo made sure we all knew the score. He said, "I don't give a damn about the myth that who ever eats the most beef will win the game. You are Michigan men, and I won't put up with any of you being gluttonous slobs. Besides if you eat too much, you won't be worth a damn at practice tomorrow. Enjoy yourself but be smart." These prime rib cuts were two inches thick, probably a couple of pounds each. We had baked potatoes, swimming in butter and sour cream, Yorkshire pudding, and spinach. It was so good that I had two plates and couldn't even look at the fudge sundaes for dessert. I was absolutely stuffed. The next day was both gross and hilarious. Just before practice, the linemen all visited the toilets. They all had consumed way more than I did. Naturally, the toilets all clogged, and the room stunk to high heaven. Some of the big guys were so proud of their artwork; they challenged us to witness the unholy sight. I felt really sorry for the maintenance crew at Citrus College where we practiced.

All of the Midwestern guys were dying to go to the beach. No matter how hard I tried to explain that it wouldn't be what they expected, I couldn't get through to them. The majority had been to Florida during the winter and had experienced the Atlantic Ocean down there where the air temperature was 85° and the water was 80°. The West Coast is not like that, especially in December and January. The air temperature may be 75° but the ocean is 60°. That difference is enough to give anyone who jumps in a new set of tonsils! But no matter how much I explained this, my teammates did not listen. It really didn't matter. These guys wanted anything except hitting through double sessions and the mountains of snow back in Ann Arbor.

At the time, we stayed at the Huntington Sheraton in Pasadena, which was a fabulous old hotel in the heart of the town. The grounds were beautiful, the service first-class, and the food was awesome. We had police escorts every day to Citrus College where we practiced. We were treated like kings. This was better than my dreams of playing for Michigan in the Rose Bowl. This was great. I wanted to bottle up every second and store it forever. But all of this was only an appetizer to the feast itself. That feast was the actual game: the Rose Bowl.

CHAPTER 62
ROSE BOWL, 1978

The 1978 Rose Bowl was my grand finale. We went to the Rose Bowl as two-time defending champions of the Big Ten. Even so it was a bittersweet experience for me. I had achieved so many of my goals and they were lofty. This was the culmination of all of them. Thinking back, my early goals had been simple. "Those who stay...," Bo's words echoed in my head, and I thought, "Just hang around and make the team." Then I pushed myself to get into a game and actually play for the great University of Michigan. Once I had done this, I wanted to make a bigger contribution to making Michigan the champions of the Big Ten. I needed to start and play all the time. Then I set goals to play in a bowl game. Ultimately, my goal was to start in a Rose Bowl game. I had done all this by my junior year, but I still wanted more. I still had a dream to score the winning touchdown in the Rose Bowl and win the National Championship. The goal to win the national title would not come true unless a miracle took place on Jan. 1, 1978. I really didn't have control over either of these final goals unless Bo deliriously started to throw the ball all over the field.

This Rose Bowl was bittersweet because I was struck with the realization that I would never, ever play football for the University of Michigan again. I was twenty-two years old and had to come to the reality that the dream I had held for the past ten years was going to end. There was nothing that anyone could do to stop it.

I think the coaches thought I was nuts because after every practice at Citrus College just outside Pasadena, California I stayed on the field when everyone was done. I didn't want time to move forward. I wanted it to stand still, just like when I had walked off the field in the Big House after we had beaten OSU. I didn't want that feeling to end.

Football had been so much of my life over the past five years. It had taken me to the highest highs I had ever experienced and to the lowest lows. Yet, the rush of playing in the Rose Bowl was, again, overwhelming.

Sure, we got to go to Lawry's for the prime rib, be the guests of honor on *The Tonight Show, Starring Johnny Carson,* and have total freedom at Disneyland for a full day. But those were just the extra curricular activities. Sure, I was set up with the Rose Bowl queen and dated her, but all that was extra noise compared to the fact that this would be my last game. If I was going to put an exclamation point on my college career, it would be with this game. I called in all my chits. I had provided every roommate with tickets for four years, and now they owed me. Now I needed them to return the favor. I gave out eighty-six tickets to friends and family to this game.

Confidence was high. We were playing Washington. Sure, they had a great quarterback in Warren Moon, but there was no way that they could stop our running attack. The first series we drove the ball right down the field. We were finally stopped inside their forty-yard line. A poor snap from center caused John Anderson to stoop for the ball as it bounced to him. The result was that the umpire called John's knee down right at our forty-five-yard line. From there the momentum was all Washington. Before we knew it we were down 24–0. It was as if the game could only go one way.

Midway through the third quarter, Bo decided that we needed to throw to get into the game. On our own twenty-four-yard line he called, "Red thirty-eight pass," which was a fake option and a quick throw to the tight end. The cornerback tried to cut me at the line of scrimmage. I jumped over him and ran straight ahead. The safety jumped the tight end, and Leach immediately saw that no one was near me. He threw a fifteen-yard pass to me, and when I looked up there was no one in front of me. I raced down the sideline, and even though the safety had the angle on me, I outran him to the end zone. Touchdown Michigan! It was a Rose Bowl record, but that was the last thing on my mind. All I remember was coming back to the sidelines and screaming at the others players that this was my home, and I was damn sure not going to be embarrassed in my home in front of my family.

The defense got fired up, and our offense caught on fire. We had a dramatic comeback. With just a few minutes to go, we had the ball on the Washington ten-yard line, and we were down 27–20. We ran a Red eighty-four pass. Stanley Edwards, a true freshman, who was playing in place of Roosevelt Smith who had been playing in the place of Harlan Huckleby, ran a swing route while I ran a hook in the end zone. Washington's cornerback jumped Stanley and the outside linebacker also ran to support him. Unfortunately, Rick threw the ball to Edwards, and as soon as he let it go, his eyes met mine as I was all alone in the end zone. The result is history. The ball bounced through Edward's hands, and instead of falling incomplete it got stuck on his shoulder pads. Stanley did a full pirouette, but the ball remained on his shoulder pads. When Stanley finally turned around and reached up for the ball, the linebacker, Michael Jackson, snatched it off his pads. The game was over. In that instant my dream ended.

My journey was over, the dream that I had ten years earlier to play for Bo and to represent the University of Michigan ended. It wasn't sad. It wasn't joyful. It was just over. Those final minutes brought an end to the greatest five years of my life. I had showed up at Bo's office with a dream, and it had come true. He had promised me that if I stayed, if I persevered, I would be a champion. He was true to his word.

When I look back on it now, I feel so many emotions. Sometimes I swell up with tears thinking about how great the experience was. Sometimes I swear at myself because I wanted to do more. But more than anything, I look at my family—where they are now and how they are perceived amongst their friends. I look at my life, and I am content. I truly believe that Bo's methods and his influence have changed my life. They are the basis for all that I am today. They are the foundation that my family is built on. I can honestly say that the greatest statement I know is, "What the mind can conceive and believe, the mind can achieve, and those who stay will be champions."

Dreams can come true as Stephenson scores in the Rose Bowl on a record breaking pass from Rick Leach

LaVergne, TN USA
21 December 2010
209762LV00002B/13/P